PRAISE FOR JEREMIE KUBICEK

Leadership Is Dead effectively reveals that lasting power and influence stems only from a servant/leader mentality based on timeless principles and true character. This remarkable book is a bold jolt of CPR to a failing heart.

—Stephen R. Covey, author of *The 7 Habits of Highly Effective People* and *The Leader in Me*

Jeremie has given a clear path to follow that will serve as a guide and a measuring stick for any leader who wants to have real and lasting influence. Take it to heart. If you want to have life-giving impact, start here.

—Dr. Henry Cloud, bestselling author of *Necessary Endings*

Jeremie Kubicek clearly shares what so many influential leaders have come to know: there's a huge difference between authority and responsibility and between influence and power.

—Seth Godin, author of *Linchpin: Are You Indispensable?*

Leadership is dead or alive, depending on how people use it. Jeremie shows us how to influence in such a way that brings *life* into organizations, and most important, into you. Don't miss this.

—Joel Manby, CEO Herschend Family Entertainment

In a world where everyone wants to be a leader, Jeremie understands that it's the influencers that change the world. This book offers you a way to move people to action and make your mark on the world. It's fast-paced, easy to act on, and most important, from the heart.

—Tim Sanders, former chief solutions officer at Yahoo! and author of *Love Is the Killer App: How to Win Business and Influence Friends*

Jeremie Kubicek delivers a unique voice on the topic of leadership, and that is not easy to do. More than that, his voice climbs off the pages as if he were standing in front of you imploring you to use your influence to help the world. Not because he is preaching, but because he has a very real desire to help you understand that leadership is more than just being in charge.

—Scott Klososky, CEO of Future Point of View and author of *The Velocity Manifesto: Harnessing Technology, Vision, and Culture to Future-Proof Your Organization* and *Enterprise Social Technology: Helping Organizations Harness the Power of Social Media, Social Networking, Social Relevance*

"Are you for me, against me, or for yourself?" That's only one of the thought-provoking questions Kubicek asks in this must-read book on true influence. This book should come with a warning: "May make you uncomfortable and reexamine your motives as you strive to be a person with trust, character, and credibility."

—Pattye Moore, chairman of the board, Red Robin Gourmet Burgers, and coauthor of *Confessions from the Corner Office: 15 Instincts That Will Help You Get There*

Where are the great leaders of our time? The world needs a new paradigm for leadership—Jeremie Kubicek has defined it. If you needed to dig a ditch, would you use a teaspoon or a bulldozer? Until now, leaders have been using a teaspoon. Every leader should read this book!

—Matthew Kelly, *New York Times* bestselling author of
The Dream Manager and president of Floyd Consulting

Get inspired. Live with intention. Make a difference. Jeremie shares "how-to" insights to manifest breakthrough leadership moments.

—Kevin Carroll, author of *Rules of the Red Rubber Ball:*
Find and Sustain Your Life's Work and founder of the Katalyst Consultancy

We need more leaders coming alive. Get ready to mark this book up.

—Brad Lomenick, president, Catalyst Movement

MAKING YOUR LEADERSHIP
COME ALIVE

MAKING YOUR LEADERSHIP
COME ALIVE

7 ACTIONS TO INCREASE YOUR INFLUENCE

JEREMIE KUBICEK

HOWARD BOOKS
A DIVISION OF SIMON & SCHUSTER, INC.
New York · Nashville · London · Toronto · Sydney · New Delhi

Howard Books
A Division of Simon & Schuster, Inc.
1230 Avenue of the Americas
New York, NY 10020

First Howard Books trade paperback edition July 2012
Previously titled *Leadership Is Dead*

HOWARD and colophon are trademarks of Simon & Schuster, Inc.

For information about special discounts for bulk purchases, please contact Simon & Schuster Special Sales at 1-866-506-1949 or business@simonandschuster.com.

The Simon & Schuster Speakers Bureau can bring authors to your live event. For more information or to book an event, contact the Simon & Schuster Speakers Bureau at 1-866-248-3049 or visit our website at www.simonspeakers.com.

Designed by Renato Stanisic

Manufactured in the United States of America.

10 9 8 7 6 5 4 3 2 1

The Library of Congress has cataloged the hardcover edition as follows:

Kubicek, Jeremie.
  Leadership is dead : how influence is reviving it / Jeremie Kubicek.
  p. cm.
1. Leadership. 2. Leadership—Psychological aspects. 3. Influence (Psychology) I. Title.
  HD57.7.K8155 2011
  658.4'092—dc22   2011008227
  ISBN 978-1-4516-1214-1
  ISBN 978-1-4516-2635-3 (pbk)
  ISBN 978-1-4516-1216-5 (ebook)

This book is dedicated to my amazing bride, Kelly.
Thank you for being alive with me. I love you!

CONTENTS

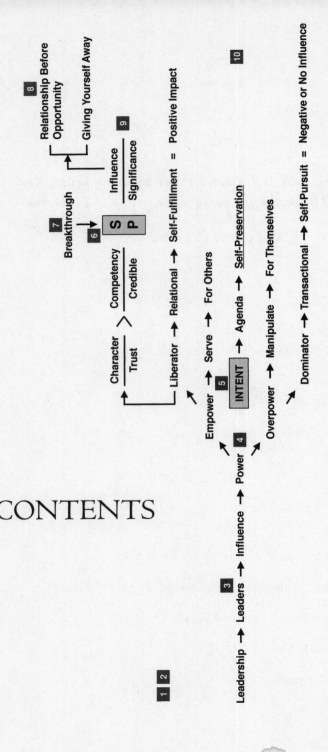

FOREWORD

One can't very well write about this book without commenting on the title.

What it really speaks to is the impending death of a tired, unproductive notion of leadership, one that has been reportedly dying for many years but has somehow managed to hang on for far too long. Well, it finally seems to be in its last throes, its death being hastened by a new economy and a new breed of free-agent followers and naïve leaders, people who have no history or vested interest in preserving the idea that power and title and—

Wait. I'll let Jeremie explain all that to you. Let me just assure those who believe that serving, supporting, and inspiring followers is more important than controlling, manipulating, and exploiting them that leadership is alive and well and should have a promising future.

What Jeremie has done here is to put together a humble, gentle, and thorough guide to embracing the right kind of leadership, the one with a future. He does so in a way that you would expect from a person who practices what he preaches, by letting you into his own life and the dramatic experiences that shaped his beliefs about living and leading.

This is not a shocking, controversial book that will be relevant for only a few months. It is a timeless reminder of something that has always been right and true, even if not always practiced. Current or aspiring leaders should read it slowly, underlining passages that speak to them, and then go back and reread it as they grow in their capacity to inspire.

I certainly hope that this book sells very well for a number of years. But I must admit that I also hope that one day in the not-too-distant future no one will need to buy it because the kind of leadership that Jeremie describes has become the standard. Because that will mean that the old model of leadership has finally been laid to rest. We can always hope.

**—Patrick Lencioni, president of the Table Group
and author of *The Five Dysfunctions of a Team***

MAKING YOUR LEADERSHIP
COME ALIVE

CHAPTER 1

DEATH OF A LEADER

Death is not a popular subject, especially when discussed within the context of leadership.

The first death to transform my life took place in my early twenties, when I was a pioneering entrepreneur in the Wild West–like city of Moscow, Russia. Car bombs and Russian Mafia hits terrorized the streets. The daily newspaper headlines made you numb to gunfights and ritual bombings.

As a young American in this setting, I felt like a cross between James Bond and John Wayne. In my mind, I was both invincible and brave. But while the business opportunity was intoxicating and the landscape thrilling, I must admit that I was a bit nervous.

My business partners and I arrived on the cold tarmac of Sheremetyevo International Airport outside of Moscow with a grand vision and eager attitudes. We were there to start a marketing consulting business and participate in the founding of an economic school. There were hundreds of leaders like us, taking risks as we hoped to establish "new" ways of doing business in a land that was very old and corrupt. Over time, we realized that there were hundreds before us who had tried to establish footholds for capitalism well before the walls of Communism had crumbled.

Paul Tatum was one of those leaders. When I moved to Moscow in 1993, two years after the dissolution of the Soviet Union, he had already built the premier commercial center for international business in the city. He was a mover and a shaker with a flashy and cocky manner. The Russians didn't know what to do with Paul. For many of the local businessmen, he was one of the first American capitalists they'd ever met.

Paul had a lot going for him: steel nerves, a string of successes, and an unmatched network of powerful political and business leaders. He had one major problem: few trusted him.

Paul had a lot going for him: steel nerves, a string of successes, and an unmatched network of powerful political and business leaders. He had one major problem: few trusted him, including many of his one hundred–plus employees. His business partners were drawn to him for his connections and financial prowess, but it seemed to me that he had few real friends because of his eccentric style.

Our company did contract work with Paul's company for a couple of years on various projects, and it was clear that self-preservation was a priority in every aspect of his life. While he didn't have many true friends, he *did* have some serious enemies.

Eventually Paul had to add a fourth layer to his three-piece suits: a bulletproof vest. The two bodyguards who accompanied him everywhere were another clue that the man had some "people issues." Few wanted to do business with him anymore, not even his former Russian partners.

I came to see that Paul had no true influence. When I'd met him, he had wealth that had bought him power in the gangsterlike city of Moscow after the Iron Curtain fell. Paul used his cash and his brash manner to manipulate and coerce his way into a power position in Moscow, but his success was short lived.

I fell in line with others who were at first intrigued and charmed by him, but then were appalled by his bold self-centeredness. I remained a friend to him longer than most, however. I was twenty-one years old when I met him. I thought Paul was drawn to the fact that my partners and I had the guts to start a business in such a challenging environment. Maybe he felt he could trust me because I was trustworthy, but if I was ever tempted to trust him, the feeling usually passed very quickly.

Paul and I met regularly for breakfast in the restaurant of a safe hotel. His bodyguards stood by the door. I listened without complaint to his self-centered banter, and I encouraged him in his business dealings. Once he felt confident in my friendship, he began to tone down the bravado and talk about his family background and his struggles in business. Paul, who'd always considered himself a maverick, was at war with his former Russian partners, and their battles were heating up. Their fight was about to turn public, and the terrible aftermath would receive international media attention.

One day, I walked down a hall from our temporary office to

come upon a bloody scene: one of his bodyguards had been stabbed. By now, Paul was under twenty-four-hour protection and working odd hours because he feared being ambushed.

I did my best to remain a friend and a positive influence on him during this period. I drew him out with questions, and we'd talk for an hour or so. Paul had isolated himself to the point that he was either working or at home. He was a virtual prisoner of his security guards, but even their vigilant efforts were not enough.

Paul was murdered on November 3, 1996, in a busy Moscow metro station near his office. His death was reported worldwide as a symbol of Russia's struggles with both its new freedoms and its lawlessness. He was believed to be the first American killed by Russian mobsters.

Paul was shot eleven times in the head and neck. He died unmarried and without many close companions. He was buried in Russia, a country he'd come to love. It was a sad story, but all too familiar in many ways.

Sadly, Paul's fierce devotion to self-preservation
and winning the game left him walled off from anyone
who could have helped him.

Paul had Domination tendencies—someone who could manipulate others and give no thought to any agenda but his own—fighting against an army of the same types of leaders. His murder would have been avoidable had he understood how to use his influence properly. Sadly, his fierce devotion to self-preservation and winning the game left him walled off from anyone who could have helped him.

I had the privilege of seeing some of the goodness in him. He unburdened himself to me and my partners, and doing so seemed to lighten his soul. At one point, he told us that ours was the only stable relationship in his life. The truth is that I really liked him, though I was not sure I trusted him. On my last meeting with Paul, he thanked me for being a good listener and asked me to pray for him. He then told me and another partner to stay clear of him from that point onward. As he said it, he motioned to the bullet-proof vest under his business suit.

After his violent death, I wished that I'd found a way to help Paul overcome his self-destructive ways. He had so much potential. He could have been a leader of great and positive influence. His death is one of the primary factors that led me to a career of working with leaders to free them of their fears and to help them reach their highest levels of positive influence. I don't think I failed Paul. If anything, I provided him a lifeline as his life was spiraling out of control. Unfortunately, he did not grasp it, nor did he understand that there were other ways—much better ways—to be a leader in business and in life.

In hindsight, I was very underprepared to serve, or save, someone of his complex nature, but I had been willing to serve as a light to someone in a very dark situation. When you are young, you meet role models for good, and role models for bad. You aspire to be like the good ones and you vow never to be like the bad ones. I learned from Paul Tatum the kind of leadership that I never wanted to practice. I saw how he died violently and alone. That was not the ending I envisioned for my life.

I had seen selfish, erratic behavior from other high-profile leaders during my international business foray. Manipulation and power maneuvers were their everyday approach. Rarely in my Russia experience did I see the type of leadership that I wanted to emulate. I watched too many leaders say one thing and then do another, and I lost respect for not just them but also for the position "leader" itself.

After decades of greed by corporate tycoons, financial moguls, and political egos, this generation is searching for authentic, selfless leadership that holds a mission higher than and outside of themselves.

This is a paramount issue for the next generation of leaders. After decades of greed by corporate tycoons, financial moguls, and political egos, this generation is searching for authentic, selfless leadership that holds a mission higher than and outside of themselves.

Paul's death was surreal. I could not process the abrupt loss of someone I'd been close to or the potential that was squandered. I reflected for many months on where this dynamic and brilliant man had gone wrong.

I have spent years analyzing leadership and influence within the role of leader. I have met and spent hours upon hours with many famous leaders—some good, some bad. In each and every meeting, I have sought to understand who they were and review their motives under the lens of desired impact and use of leadership. It is vitally important to me that leadership is no longer squandered or abused. This dedicated effort has taken almost a decade.

Before I knew it, I would suddenly be forced to reflect on my own leadership through a dramatic event. Almost ten years after Paul's tragedy, everything would change.

CHAPTER 2

MY DEATH AND MY NEW LIFE

My death had never entered my mind until the night of September 22, 2002.

As a young business leader, I rarely thought about death. I was too focused on life. My wife and kids were amazing. My business ventures were fun and, for the most part, successful. The future seemed so bright that I could only look forward to an even more fulfilling life.

On that September night, though, my perspective changed forever, and the concept for this book was born.

I'd never realized it before, but September is a risky time to be in Cancún, Mexico. As much as tourists love it, so do hurricanes. Resorts entice would-be travelers during hurricane season with special packages. They don't mention the extra added attraction of 130-mile-per-hour winds, driving rain, flooding, and power outages. My wife and I took the bait. We were joined by our friends Ryan and Carmel. We were in desperate need of a vacation, as I'd just quit a good job to start my dream company, and this trip was a pause before the storm of a start-up. Or so we'd thought.

When a hurricane enters a resort's radius, plywood and tarps seem to board up buildings and their windows as if by magic. We were stunned at the transformation of our open-aired paradise into a sealed fortress. Our hosts gave us the option of staying in the darkened hotel or fleeing inland to accommodations that were less on the front line of the hurricane but a few stars short of a Red Roof Inn. We chose to move inland for safety's sake. Little did we know that the city had its own substantial dangers.

Cancún was locking down for a storm, but we refused to give up on our vacation. The beach and pool weren't an option, so we headed for a movie, figuring that if we had to be in a dark, windowless place, it might as well have entertainment and popcorn. We chose a theater showing M. Night Shyamalan's *Signs*. The movie features aliens and some scary scenes, but at its heart, it is a story of faith restored. Entertaining and sometimes frightening, the film was a great distraction from the first storm bands drenching our resort getaway. In the film, actor Mel Gibson loses his wife in a traffic accident, a tragedy that leads him to give up on his faith in God. Later he nearly loses his son but instead experiences a miracle. This moment and others restore his belief and trust in God.

I tend to analyze movies, and this one was ripe for contemplation. As we left the theater, I began breaking down the story scene by scene in my mind. I was consumed by certain decisions made by the characters, and I paid little attention to the fact that we were swimming through a downpour as we hailed a cab.

The driver informed us that we had about two hours before Isidore, a category 3 hurricane, would descend in its full fury. We were being driven through a torrential downpour. I'd grown up in central Oklahoma, in the middle of "Tornado Alley," but I had never seen rain fall in such heavy sheets. Our little Fiat taxi was buffeted about by the storm like a row boat in a sea squall. I was in the front passenger seat, with Kelly, Ryan, and Carmel in back. My wife sat directly behind me.

For some reason, I didn't fasten my seatbelt. Why do we feel any safer in taxis than in our own cars? With the movie still playing in my mind, I was wondering if I would respond as Mel Gibson had if something tragic should happen to Kelly or to our kids. As we sped through the besieged Mexican resort town, still two miles from our new hotel, the taxi's windshield wipers seemed to give up in their battle with the pounding rain. The storm had grown so intense that I said a little prayer that also reflected fears sparked by the movie's plot.

God, if anything happens to Kelly, I want you to know I will trust you. I won't stop believing in you. If anything happens to my kids, Addison, Will, or Kate, I will trust you. I won't stop believing in you.

I don't know whether the storm compounded my fears from the movie, or whether the movie made the storm seem more threatening. I just felt overwhelmed in that instant and added one final thought to my prayer: And, God, if anything ever happens to me, I want you to know that I will trust you!

I took momentary comfort in noting that Kelly and Carmel did not seem to share my anxiety. They were talking about their purchases in the marketplace that afternoon. Kelly was excited about a gift she had bought for her mother. I took that as a sign that despite the fierce weather, my wife was in control of her emotions.

The next thing I heard was Kelly screaming "Watch out!"

Our taxi had entered an intersection directly in front of our hotel. A very bright set of headlights flashed in my eyes, blinding me. There was a horrendous, metallic explosion. Then darkness, the rain, and the smell of spilled fuel.

The passenger side of our taxi had been split open by the vehicle of a drunk driver. I was crushed at impact.

The passenger side of our taxi had been split open by the vehicle of a drunk driver. I was crushed at impact.

Since that life-changing day, I've heard other survivors of horrific car accidents describe the "death scream" that roars from you as pain engulfs you like a ravenous flame. I returned to consciousness, and I felt as though I was observing all of this from outside my body. I could see broken glass and the steam rising from the other car, which rested ominously near the mangled taxi. Hurricane Isidore refused to pause for our ugly wreck.

I couldn't feel my legs, but tiny knives were stabbing me in the back. I could hear my own screams and I could "hear" myself think as Ryan, Carmel, and Kelly scrambled to free themselves so they could assist me.

In shock and barely able to suck air into my lungs, I was already feeling the surge of deep pain in sharp waves. My conscious mind struggled to fathom what had just occurred, while my body convulsed in response.

The drunk driver's car had pinned me against the taxi driver's seat, snapping and crushing my ribs, and forcing my sternum to nearly explode from my chest.

I took the brunt of the impact. My wife had deep shoulder

bruises, but, thankfully, she and the others in the backseat were spared serious injuries.

I was still trapped in the car when the thought came: *I am so glad it was me! I am so glad it was me!* I felt that I'd prepared myself for my injuries in my conversation with God just prior to the collision. Even with the pain growing more intense, I once again told God that I trusted Him. Still, I was frightened, especially when I realized that I couldn't move my legs. I feared that I'd been paralyzed.

Suddenly, despite my pain and fear, the onslaught of the powerful hurricane, and the chaos of the car crash and its aftermath, I felt at peace. God was with me in those moments—I could feel it—as we waited for an ambulance to make it through the storm. In that time span, my experience ranged from crippling pain to flashes of hope.

Kelly was trying to make me comfortable. I kept telling her that I couldn't feel my legs. The stabbing pains in my back were unrelenting. I could barely breathe, which was also a problem. I could not get air into my lungs. The harder I tried, the less air I could take in.

Is this it? Is this the way I die? In a taxi? In a hurricane? In Mexico?

Kelly saw the fear in my eyes and soothed me with her loving gaze. She gently stroked my hair and said, "I know. Help is on the way. It will be okay." Later she would tell me that in that moment she feared that I would not survive.

Death seemed like a real possibility to me, too. My internal conversation with God took a more serious turn.

God, was I the man you wanted me to be?

My relationship with God played out in my mind: I saw myself at ten years old when I first dreamed of Him; at thirteen, when I really began to understand who He was; eighteen years old and in college, which was when I began to understand who *I* was; twenty-one, when I lived overseas and relied on Him at every level. And so on, throughout my life. This went on for several minutes, each picture a scene of my life answering the very question I had just asked.

Then came the next question: *God, was I the husband you wanted me to be?*

Again, life pictures were presented as I watched my bride walk with me through the years of our marriage. I envisioned us on our wedding day, walking across the bridge near her parents' house to say our vows. I saw us as newlyweds, always gazing into each other's eyes. Then the years sped past with the births of our children and the blossoming of our life as a family. These life pictures were vibrant and powerful. Despite my pain, I was carried away with emotion as those scenes played out in my mind.

The final question dealt with my kids: *God, was I the father you wanted me to be?*

My children's faces appeared to me: Addison, Will, and Kate beamed at me, filling me with sweet joy and peace. I saw us at play together, doing homework together, at their games and school plays, and at church. God was revealing to me my love for my kids, and a rush of peace came to counter some of the agony wracking my body.

I opened my eyes and felt relieved to see Kelly again, but my lungs ached for lack of air and my body was convulsing. I was fading into unconsciousness, and I feared that if I closed my eyes, I would never see my wife again.

Kelly had no idea of my inner conversation with God when she said tenderly, "Jeremie, I want you to know you are God's man; you are a great husband; and you are a great daddy!"

Her words sent this strange wave of relief through my body. *You can let go now*, I thought. My wife and my God had given me permission to sign off. I was only thirty years old, yet I had already experienced an amazing life filled with love, faith, and adventure. I'd created businesses and formed wonderful partnerships while traveling the world, but what really mattered in that moment, and ever since, is that I was a godly man, a good husband, and a good father. All the striving could stop as I heard who I really was.

On September 22, at approximately ten thirty at night, on the rain-soaked streets of Cancún, Mexico, I took my last breath, and the world faded from view. They say that the gift of sound is the final function to shut down at death, and that appeared to hold true in my case. I can remember fading out visually but still hearing everything around me quite clearly.

Then there was silence, and I was gone. Or so I thought.

I survived despite all indications to the contrary. I did not experience one miracle; I experienced several—on that night and throughout the next week. Many lives were changed beyond my own, as those who loved me and cared for me witnessed so many miraculous events.

While I very much appreciate still being on this earth, the journey from near death back to a full life was often painful. I suffered through one medical emergency after another. The first was in a hurricane-battered Mexican hospital with no running water and sporadic electricity. What was supposed to have been a four-day, all-inclusive vacation turned into an eleven-day nightmare. We would have stayed longer to recover had another hurricane threat not sent me on a strategic flight home despite the risk of aggravating my surgical wounds and internal bleeding. By then, however, we had already faced death several times as doctors in the poorly equipped hospital worked to repair my badly damaged internal organs. While I wouldn't wish the physical and emotional pain I experienced on anyone, I did come away from this nightmare a better man, and a much better leader. In fact, one of my favorite songs is "Hello Hurricane" by the band Switchfoot. It goes like this:

> Hello hurricane, you're not enough
> Hello hurricane, you can't silence my love

That's my song. Strange as it may seem, this tortuous experience proved to be a blessing in many ways. As a result of that near-fatal accident, I had a breakthrough—many, actually. I had the privilege of asking the most important questions that human beings can ask.

I came to fully comprehend the influence I have on the lives of others, and the impact their lives have on me.

Every answer I needed came to me during my suffering and recovery. I came to fully comprehend the influence I have on the lives of others, and the impact their lives have on me.

Being crushed in a Mexican cab rather cruelly and abruptly rearranged a few of my body parts, but it also substantially changed my thinking in ways that have marked my life and career ever since.

I went to Cancún to recharge my batteries before starting a

company that I hoped would change the business world. I left there a changed man: a bit broken, but better in that I had new perspective about the importance of life.

Bucket List

Let me explain more deeply how my death affected my leadership. I've always had a bucket list of things I wanted to accomplish. When I was twenty years old, I set goals to hit by the time I was forty. The list included living overseas, starting a company, serving as CEO of an influential company, traveling the world, and other personal goals.

By the age of thirty, I'd accomplished most of the items on my list.

Over time, I added to my bucket list goals such as launching an Internet-based company, traveling with my wife and kids, and writing a book. By the age of thirty, I'd accomplished most of the items on my list. I had cofounded a company in Russia at the age of twenty-one. I had become vice president of a large merchandising company. I'd participated in a national acquisition roll-up. I'd started two Internet ventures, and I'd created an inspiring new type of company in GiANT that helps leaders and companies grow exponentially.

My extroverted personality naturally connects with people, and my ambitious entrepreneurial drive uncovers opportunities almost weekly. My leadership style was aggressive. Looking back, I could confidently say that I was addicted to accomplishment and the approval those accomplishments brought from others. This style of leadership could run roughshod over people who couldn't keep up with me.

Don't get me wrong: most everyone who knew me would have said I was a good guy prior to my accident. In fact, I would say that I was very mission driven. My moral compass was sturdy, and so was my intent. I genuinely desired the best for others and myself. God simply reset my paradigm for living and for leading. My religious zeal was impacted by the living God. My view of life was affected by a view of death. Priorities were challenged and resolved.

For the first time in my life, I got to actually experience how big God is. Before the accident, I was set in my ways of how God operated and how He didn't. When people had questions, I had the answers—I was a bit of a know-it-all when it came to life and death. I was well read, and so, intellectually, I felt like I could address all things in the "How God works" category. My assertive knowledge was probably why I was also chosen to lead in most situations.

One movie, one hurricane, and one run-in with a drunk driver changed all of that. I watched my view of God broaden in an instant when I asked and He answered. God realigned my priorities from mere accomplishments to Him, my wife, and my kids. He showed me that He could perform miracles and could take care of me without my assistance.

In my "death," I actually had an encounter with God and took the needed hit in order to die by my own leadership style. It was replaced by a lifestyle centered on a stronger belief in what God could do. The experience in the taxi cab and subsequent miracles in the outdated Mexican hospital, however, brought the gift of *enlivenment*. I had been influenced by many things that week, and my enlightenment and my enlivenment emerged to awaken the real me.

My seeming death actually became a revived life with a new view of leading others.

Immediately after the accident and throughout my initial recovery, I realized that keeping a bucket list was too limiting, since my life was no longer a solitary journey. I had a family, and it was no longer all about me and what I wanted. Even more, I was able to begin anew before we started GiANT. What a gift. I had gained perspective on both living and leading—everything became new.

A few weeks after my recovery, I painfully walked into our brand-new albeit modest office with wrapped ribs and a surgical scar that most men would brag about. My business partner, Matthew Myers, and I began thinking differently about business and about leadership. We set strong goals from this refined perspective. We established fresh approaches for serving customers, treating employees, and leading initiatives. My soul felt renewed, even though my body was still broken.

I'd been liberated from a self-centered leadership style into a broader view of influence. The concept of leadership came alive again as I saw that it was not about status or money or accomplishment. I began to look at leadership as a vehicle to influence people and have a positive impact upon them. I was blessed to see the end of my life long before it actually ended. In that moment, a change was initiated that would play out over several years, and, in fact, I am still discovering the power of that breakthrough every day.

Since that rainy September night, my leadership style has changed to become much more focused on others. I have chosen to serve the interests of others before seeking opportunities for myself. I invest first in their dreams and find that I am more excited about their journey than even my own. Make no mistake: I am still a business guy. In fact, I am still very aggressive and entrepreneurial. But my priorities and perspective were reset that fateful night in Mexico. As a young leader I began to come alive.

CHAPTER 3

WHY SOME LEADERS ARE DEAD

Most of us carry a mixed bag of emotions when it comes to leadership. We see those who claim to be leaders but don't "walk the walk," and we have known leaders who have won us over with their integrity.

In my view, leadership is currently strained because far too many leaders have abused their positions and lost their moral bearings. Traditional leadership principles, and the traditional training of those principles, apparently do not work in the modern world. Greed, selfishness, corruption, and self-preservation have prevailed time and time again in recent years, often to devastating effect. From the banking industry collapse to corporate greed, these leaders have abandoned all long-term responsibility and discipline in favor of short-term gains. The runaway greed of Wall Street's leadership, skyrocketing salaries for corporate executives, and unkept promises from political leaders have left most people feeling betrayed and jilted. Not only do we not trust our leaders, but in many cases, employees are becoming victims of these unresponsive leaders.

Consequently, most leaders are now viewed with cynicism and skepticism, and many have lost the trust of those they are supposed to inspire and motivate. This is true not only in public leadership positions but also in rank-and-file leadership in both large and small organizations throughout America. Main Street leadership suffers from the same greed, self-preservation, and unresponsiveness as Wall Street. I have witnessed it firsthand as our company talks with leaders weekly who are dealing with wide-scale leadership erosion.

True empowering leadership can be revived if we are willing to embrace a few core concepts:

- We must understand what the role of leadership is and what it is not.
- We must be willing to explore the inner world of leadership—things such as intent, power, and motive.
- Influence needs to be recognized as the engine of true leadership.
- Leaders must understand how to influence, not simply how to lead.

Influence is the most potent and underutilized professional resource on the planet.

Anyone can make an impact on others. You don't need great wealth or vast experience to help another person. You don't need massive power or a prominent position to lead positive change in an organization. You need only influence: the most potent and underutilized professional resource on the planet.

It is influence that makes true leadership come to life. Where manipulation typically wounds, influence energizes. To be influential requires that we shed the fears and self-preservation instincts that hold us back.

Self-Preservation as Self-Destruction

Self-preservation has no place in the mind of a modern leader; at least not if he or she expects anyone to follow. Today's leaders must break down any walls of self-preservation. They must be willing to sacrifice their own security to reach and inspire others. The amazing paradox is that the more you give away, the more everyone receives, including you: more success, more significance, and more security. Contrary to the "greed is good" mentality that has permeated leadership at so many levels in recent times, the greatest strategy for business success and personal fulfillment is not based upon getting all you can. Instead it is centered upon giving all you can.

The greatest strategy for business success and
personal fulfillment is not based upon getting all you can.
Instead it is centered upon giving all you can.

Fears and insecurities plague us all. Fight-or-flight survival instincts are triggered by those fears and insecurities. Sometimes, though, self-preservation can become self-defeating. We build walls that keep others out and hold us back. We become so guarded, so focused on protecting our ideas, our status, and our reputations, that we always play it safe, avoid risk, and never reach out beyond our most trusted and loyal circle.

This is self-preservation run amok: while your walls protect you, they also restrict you and your ability to influence others. Your coworkers, team members, and direct reports will not consistently listen to you, buy into you, or go to battle for you unless they believe that you are invested in their interests and needs too. The more those around you sense that you are only looking out for number one, the less interested they'll be in serving as your number two, three, four, or five.

You may be the designated leader according to your job title, but without true influence, you'll have little impact. Business interactions without influence are merely transactional. They never evolve beyond buying, selling, and bartering. Deals might be consummated and tasks might be completed, but lives remain the same. If there is an impact, it is as fleeting as that new-car smell.

Sadly, most business relationships fall—and I do mean *fall*—into this category: they wax and wane on persuasion and power. They too are ephemeral. There is no foundation of trust and mutual respect, and so there is nothing of substance to build upon. The zeitgeist of corporate responsibility demands an approach to business based on deeper levels of trust and pay-it-forward relationships.

Business leaders with keenly developed powers of influence operate at a higher level than those who merely seek to con-

vince, coerce, and close deals . . . Their interactions go beyond
transactions; they build relationships that change the world.

Business leaders with keenly developed powers of influence operate at a higher level than those who merely seek to convince, coerce, and close deals. They chart a course into deeper waters. Their interactions go beyond transactions; they build relationships that change the world.

Historical Perspective

For more than one hundred years, business leadership models have been based on organizational management techniques developed during the industrial revolution. The rise of large organizations required a systematic hierarchy and chain-of-command processes that executed orders in almost assembly-line fashion. Most of these corporations were large manufacturers. The leadership and management models that evolved were designed for workplaces in which scores of employees were assigned to small organizational groups to facilitate mass production.

Our world of work has changed dramatically in recent decades, and so the success of our nation demands a new type of leader and new approaches to leadership itself.

The US military has recognized this and responded in remarkable fashion. Historically, the military's rules of engagement were based on a command-and-control management style that was itself rooted in the industrial age. Wars were fought nation against nation, in an industrially organized fashion. The enemy was always clearly defined. World War II pitted the Allies against the Axis powers. The Cold War pitted the Soviets against the West.

That model for warfare was changed forever one Tuesday morning in the fall of 2001. The September 11, 2001, terrorist assault on US targets was a call to arms on a new battlefield, one in which the US military was pitted against an ideology rather than another nation.

Our military leaders are worthy of great respect. I have had the privilege of being with some outstanding officers at the US Army's leadership headquarters in Fort Leavenworth, Kansas. I've even had the opportunity to develop a friendship with one particular leader. His responsibilities as a lieutenant general include leadership of over one hundred thousand officers and personnel. His experience includes training in Afghanistan, among other responsibilities.

He is one of my heroes. I've learned a great deal from him in our discussions. At one meeting, I asked the general about changes in the military's traditional approach to leadership since the September 11, 2001, terrorist attacks.

He told me that the US Army is trained to fight for peace, to make things safer and better. He said when 9/11 happened, a great shift occurred. People used to think that the US Army was a powerful, destructive force, but now they must balance two things: a clenched fist to take down opposition and an open hand to lend assistance and render aid.

He went on to describe the surreal experience of American soldiers responding to sniper fire in a hostile area, while at the same time, one mile away, their fellow soldiers were digging a well so the locals no longer had to walk a half mile for fresh water. The clenched fist and openhanded approach to military engagement has affected recruiting, leader development, and the entire training process.

Imagine how difficult it must have been to transform the US military's approach to war-fighting in Iraq and Afghanistan. Yet this lieutenant general said that this mission has been accomplished.

He told me that the military can win battles. It knows how to do that well. However, the military must also win at peace. That takes leadership to a whole new level.

The military must now work with diplomats and local leaders more than ever before. The new philosophy of the US Army demands that soldiers be trained in both the use of force and the more benevolent use of influence. Military leaders now train their young recruits to be both warriors and cultural connectors, forces of destruction and forces for construction.

The best leadership minds are studying the implications of influence, both positive and negative. Today's leaders understand the cause and effect of power. They know how to train leaders to empower others so they can deal with the new dynamics confronting our world.

In similar dramatic fashion, the landscape of work has shifted. Technology has changed the game. Social media and new devices are transforming communication, computers have greatly altered work habits, and the ease of global trade has affected worldwide commerce. Computer- and Internet-savvy members of the "creative class" have changed the rules of engagement in the workplace.

Both leadership and the leader must adapt or risk becoming irrelevant. This is the new reality in the world of work. Social change occurs faster than ever before due to global networks that provide instant access to information. This dynamic environment makes some people skeptical until there is proof that the new technology is truly valuable. Leadership is no different. Our expectations for authenticity have risen, while all too often our leaders perform below our high expectations.

The Change in Leadership Culture

Change in a leader can inspire change around the world. My experience in Mexico and the breakthrough it triggered changed my world, which in turn affected my life, my family, and my business. The perspective on leadership I'd long had died in that Cancún taxi cab. The revelation I experienced can be stated simply: I realized that positive leadership occurs not by "leading" others but rather by influencing them.

America's traditional concept of leadership is under challenge. The people of the United States are communicating more clearly than ever their frustration with hypocritical leadership. Companies are seeing the need to create a new style of leadership culture rather than the rote top-down style of past decades.

Transformations in the way we work and where we work have forced adjustments in management styles and in the way managers communicate with employees and contractors. Nearly every industry has had to adapt in some way as the traditional corporate and industrial workplace models have been rendered ineffective or unworkable.

These wholesale shifts in the way that Americans work have inspired new approaches to leadership. Today's most dynamic leaders have discarded the power hungry command-and-control model and embraced one in which they aspire more to influence and impact those in their workforces. For these reformers, *leadership* is a verb rather than a noun. It is a vehicle for appropriate change, not the end goal.

When I asked a twentysomething leader at Catalyst West—one of our events within the Catalyst brand focused on the under-forty-year-old leader—to describe the difference between the old and new models of leadership, he said, "Leadership in the past was a bunch of people who worked in committees and had a bunch of rules of order. I think our generation is more about influence."

While every generation breaks away from the practices of previous generations at some level, the dramatic transition from the industrial revolution to the technological age has resulted in radical changes in how this new generation views and approaches leadership.

Probably the best example of this in the early twenty-first century is Ford Motor Company. The auto giant was the benchmark for industrial expertise for most of the twentieth century. Time changes all things, however, and so the need for Ford to adapt became evident over the past decade or two. President and CEO Alan Mulally, who joined the company in 2006, was the change agent that Ford needed to overhaul tired systems with vibrant new energy.

Mulally's ingenuity has been seen in virtually all areas of the company, from the preparation for economic downturns to the emphasis on quality standards to the way dealer relations are handled—nothing has gone unnoticed. The results are being seen in excellence and innovation that is turning heads with Americans who in the past may have never looked twice at a Ford vehicle. This commitment to doing things right has caused them to overhaul practices, systems, and personnel to become relevant again.

That is what influential leaders do. They make things that were dead come alive.

Because of this dynamic reversal, I believe that you will see Ford set up for success for the next fifty years. The cynicism and rust of an old leadership culture is being replaced with a relevant responsiveness that has never been seen in Detroit. The desire to influence and impact customers is changing leadership within Ford with an obvious outward focus. Ford represents a new style of leadership that is practical to watch and observe.

Practical Influence

Great leaders are always needed, now more than ever, but today's executives must understand the roots of influence and the benevolent use of power if they hope to exert a positive impact on their work forces.

Collin Sewell understands influence. His team lives under his empowering leadership style daily. Collin leads one of the most successful Ford dealerships in America: Sewell Ford, in Odessa, Texas. After spending a day with his team, I was overwhelmed by the empowering culture that Collin had developed.

Collin shared with me how it took him years to make leadership come alive, and mostly within himself. He began to understand that leadership was not about him but about the opportunity to influence others. Today you can see the life within his organization. Every employee I spoke with had a well-defined role that he or she understood in depth. Collin has built a system of empowerment in which each team member understands that individual success and failure also impacts other teammates and the company as a whole.

The culture of true influence starts with Collin. He sets the tone. Collin is intense, because his vision is so strong. He believes in transformation, and he understands the implications of positive impact. I met one employee after another who seemed to revere and respect him because Collin "walks the walk." He empowers because he has been empowered. He understands that empowered people feel free to accept responsibility, which allows them to grow and achieve more than they may have dreamed possible.

One of Collin's team leaders, named "Coach," shared with me, "I am free to be me. Mr. Sewell hired me to lead, and that is what I do. I get to use my day job to help people and serve them. I also get to train young kids to do things they have never been trained to do."

His enthusiasm was contagious, and so is influence. If the leader at the top of an organization makes it known that his goal is to help others succeed, the ripple effect has a positive influence on the entire team. Leadership is alive and well at Sewell Ford.

Personal Perspective

The need for true influence and evolved leadership is clear and evident. We all need great leaders to inspire and motivate us to perform at peak levels. Every person wants to feel free to put his or her gifts to the highest use. Each of us wants to be valued and treated with respect.

Yet all too often our leaders fall short of those expectations. A me-first mentality prevails and permeates our culture. This can be traced to broken families and high divorce rates that have spawned generations of men and women who have difficulty connecting with others and being authentic. Many grew up observing that adult actions rarely matched their words.

Too often today, individuals attempt to make "withdrawals" from relationships without first having made any "deposits."

After nearly a decade at the helm of an organization focused on leader development, I am still amazed that many who aspire to be leaders have such a poor understanding of that role or what true leadership requires.

I recently received a call from an old acquaintance who knew that I was in the business of training leaders. He wanted me to promote his "leadership" thoughts.

"Jeremie, old friend," he began. "How are you? Good, good. Say, listen, I know you are in the leadership business, and, well, quite frankly, I believe I have what it takes to be the next leader to leaders."

I asked him to tell me more.

"Well, you see, I am a leader. I have always been a leader. People do what I say. I get things done because I know how to influence people. My leadership principles are bold and will help people do what I do."

He then noted, however, that he'd left his job recently because "I was set up for failure. They didn't listen. I knew what to do, but they wouldn't change. That is when I left. That is why we need the leadership principles I have created, so people will become better leaders."

This longtime acquaintance had it all wrong, from my point of view. He called himself a leader, yet he had no grasp of how to influence others in a positive way. He certainly didn't influence *me* with his self-serving approach. When I turned down his request for my business to promote him as a leadership trainer, he was flabbergasted.

"I thought you were a leadership guy," he said.

That I am, but in my view, leadership should never be a me-first proposition. I believe that anyone who aspires to be a good and positive leader must embrace certain principles and standards in today's world of work.

To help define my view of a new paradigm for leadership, I will be providing some language and criteria that will help you become a more effective leader and a positive influencer in the lives of others. My goal is to also give you a framework for building upon your strengths and eliminating your weaknesses so that you can fulfill your potential as an effective, life-changing leader.

Leadership Styles

Effective leadership is built upon forging win-win relationships with active influence. Yet it is about more than mere collaboration. A leader highlights the path, models the principles and values of a group, or a department, or an entire organization, and encourages those who follow in pursuit of their clearly designated goals.

Some leaders are better at one than the other. I have known great leaders who light brilliant paths but are less strong in encouraging follow-through. Others, meanwhile, are superb in creating a strong principle-based leadership culture but less overt in communicating the vision. The best leaders are those who have simplified it down to relationships. When that occurs, grace for the leader's failings are given as much as grace for the minor failings of employees.

To be an effective, respected, and positive force for change, today's leaders must overcome our cultural tendencies toward narcissism and self-centeredness. We live in a society that is too often enamored of celebrity, outward appearance, and material wealth. In such an environment, the temptation is to emphasize perception over reality, style over substance, words over actions. Whole industries have arisen to serve this culture of narcissism, from cosmetic surgery clinics to custom clothing designers.

Yet most people will tell you that they value leaders who demonstrate substance over style, and action over words. We may gawk at the perfectly coiffed and the expensively clad, but we are more drawn to follow the authentic person comfortable with herself, open, engaging, and invested in our success as well as her own.

So how do you develop your leadership style? From the inside out. You first lead by example. Who you are, your values, your beliefs, how you treat others; those attributes say more than anything you can wear, drive, or mortgage. In the same way that clothing communicates the fashion sense of an individual, the actions of a leader provide insights into leadership style. Most respected and even revered leaders attract followers because of who they are, what they stand for, and how they relate to and influence others. They rarely resort to coercion or intimidation.

You can also mold your leadership style by observing leaders that you admire and emulating them. We find our clothing styles by watching others and trying things on to see if we like them or not. We build a wardrobe by selecting clothing that suits us and feels comfortable. Of course, some of us—sorry, Dad—find a style and never change it. My father refuses to wear anything but white tennis shoes because "that's what I've always worn." That's a risky approach to leadership. Since a leader's role is to be at the forefront of change, being left behind is a bad career move.

For many years, employees of IBM, which once dominated the computer market, were known for always wearing look-alike dark blue suits, white shirts, and dark ties. The corporate uniform at Big Blue reflected a management style that was all but etched in stone.

Then along came the clever techies in jeans and T-shirts at Apple, Dell, and Hewlett-Packard, who ran off with the personal computer market while IBM stubbornly clung to its massive mainframes.

Leaders who refuse to change their leadership style risk being left behind by those who are quicker on their feet, more flexible, and forward thinking. It's also true that if you fall into a pattern of leadership that serves your purpose but not the purposes of those under your command, you may find yourself in front of an empty room. That is why I advocate leadership through influence. If influence is your style, you have no choice but to stay in touch and work from the win-win position.

One of our early CEO clients admitted to me years ago that he felt "irrelevant" to his young staff. This top executive confided that he'd never had a mentor of his own and that he'd risen to his high position mostly by trying not to repeat the mistakes of bad leaders he'd observed on his way up. The problem with this approach was that he'd never developed his own identity as a leader. In confidential interviews, his employees told me that they didn't know him or what he stood for, and that he lacked consistency, flip-flopping in his management styles and his moods from day to day and from one situation to the next.

This leader's style was defined solely by what he *didn't* want to be. This is akin to someone trying to achieve sainthood simply by avoiding mistakes. There's more to it than just that. While learning from other people's mistakes is a valuable practice, it's not much of a leadership strategy. I advised this executive to hire a chief operating officer to run the business day to day while he focused on developing his own management persona. Today he is a consistent and respected leader because he defined what he wants for himself, for his company, and for his team.

Is it important to have a well-defined leadership style? Think of the leaders who stand out in your mind. Is it difficult for you to define their styles of leading? What about each of these noted leaders; can you identify each with a particular style?

- Steve Jobs, CEO of Apple
- President Barack Obama
- Donald Trump
- Late President Ronald Reagan
- Your boss
- You

Whatever you may think of each one, you have to admit that his leadership style is well defined. The late President Reagan developed as a leader of influence through superior communication rather than as a command-and-control leader, because he earned his stripes during seven terms as the elected president of the Screen Actors Guild. There he had to build consensus and mutually beneficial alliances to advance his platforms. That, along with his service as governor of California, served him well later as president of the United States when he had to deal with Congress and with world leaders.

President Reagan was so skillful at connecting with others that even those who disagreed with his policies found him to be engaging and likable, which helped him influence them despite their reservations. In contrast, the late President Richard Nixon, who lacked personal warmth and communication skills, often alienated even those who admired his intellect and his platform.

You may be brilliant and full of great ideas, but you can lead only if others are willing to follow you. To enlist their support and cooperation, you need to convince them that their goals are aligned with your own and that you wish to influence them for their own benefit. This sort of leader provides hope by investing in the dreams of those willing to follow. This leadership style is about understanding yourself and knowing how to arrange your strengths to complement those of your team members.

Not All Leadership Is Equal

As an entrepreneur, I have learned that not all money is equal. A loan or investment always has strings attached, and sometimes those strings can feel like a noose around your neck. One type of loan is different from the next. While the dollar amount may be the same, the terms are different with each deal and with each lender.

The same applies to leadership. Therefore, it would benefit us to understand the nuances of leadership. Please note that the following list doesn't mean to imply that one leadership position is preferable to another but that leaders' priorities may conform to the size and structure of their organization.

- The Public Corporate Leader—Leadership in a public company means handling the pressure of hitting quarterly numbers to keep stockholders happy. The pressure of this role forces the majority of public company CEOs and the managers under them to focus primarily on investor perception, short-term results, and crisis management at the expense of long-term investment.

- The Private CEO Leader—Leadership for a top executive in a private company means more control and influence on the company's culture than for the leaders of publicly held companies. Private company leaders maintain more control over their financials, and so they tend to exert a powerful influence on their employees.
- The Small Business Leader—Leadership to a small business leader means meeting the demands of the biweekly payroll and cash flow, which does not allow for significant investment in leadership development. Leadership often is delivered on the fly, and because these leaders wear multiple hats, they often face pressures that limit their ability to plan for long-term leadership growth.
- The Division Leader—Leadership inside a large corporation is often more about managing political and personal agendas than anything else. The fear of losing power and the desire for promotion often lead to posturing and maneuvering within the organization, which creates a "survivor" or "every man for himself" environment.
- The Nonprofit Leader—To the nonprofit leader, leadership entails handling the board of directors appropriately, while overseeing the leadership teams. This approach often places more emphasis on consensus building and charismatic vision casting to secure donors and other sources of funding.
- The Civic Leader—Leadership within city, state, or federal government demands tackling large bureaucratic game playing and managing key constituents. Regulations, red tape, public oversight, and budget limitations affect the civic leader's ability to move swiftly and decisively.

- The Political Leader—Leadership to the politician is typically about elections and fund-raising while overseeing his or her elected duties. The elected leader is often consumed with the need to appease financial supporters, keep constituents happy, and dance with (or around) the news media. Manipulative maneuvering is often a negative approach, while consensus building is more positive.
- The Church Leader—Leadership to a church leader is about managing a staff of volunteers and overseeing church finances while serving as a spiritual role model, guide, and counselor. This presents many challenges. The church leader has many hats to wear and usually many overseers and critics. Charismatic leadership is often practiced, as well as consensus building.
- The Family Leader—Leadership in the home means running a household and taking care of personal responsibilities and those of the family. Parental responsibilities and relationships with the children and the spouse are primary concerns.

Leadership means different things to different people. The nuances of each are amazing. To take it a step further, it is important to understand the specific differences of leadership within categories, especially as you communicate across industries or roles:

- Founders Compared to Hired Guns—The founder is usually heavily invested personally and financially in the success of his business. Because of this, founders tend to demand greater control than hired CEOs, who tend to delegate more responsibilities.

- Small Companies Compared to Large Companies—Large companies generally have more resources. Small companies are more nimble. Thus, the leadership approach required may differ.
- Frontline Views Compared to Headquarters View—Frontline leaders are engaged day to day with customers and focus on short-term strategies. As a result, they can lose sight of long-term objectives. Headquarters-based leaders rely more on secondhand reports about customers while focusing on long-term plans. They may lose their connection to the customer.

Many factors shape leaders and their style of leadership. Take a moment to examine your own role as a leader and the factors that influence how you approach your position.

- What sort of leaders did you observe growing up?
- What types of leaders have you worked for? How did you respond to their styles of leadership?
- How many different types of organizations have you worked in? (Corporate? Private? Government? Nonprofit? Large? Small?)

Every leader's personal style is affected by past experiences with work leaders, church leaders, and parents or guardians. To improve as a leader, we must understand where we have come from and the type of environment we are in today.

Where Leaders Begin

Every leader has to start somewhere. For some of us, our parents modeled great leadership and/or poor leadership. From our first boss to our current leaders, we all begin somewhere.

I view leadership culture as a seedbed. Each leader is a seed planted in that seedbed. The seed, or leader, needs several things in order to grow:

1. Good soil. *Where* leaders are planted matters. A lot of people are planted in tough soil and never experience the growth that they could. The environment is almost impossible to grow properly. Conversely, great soil brings out the most in a person, which allows them to grow.
2. Enough water. Without the basic tools, it is impossible to grow. I am amazed at how few leaders help younger leaders with the basics of leading. We all need water.
3. Nutrients/fertilizer. Nutrients to leaders are specific things they need to grow in their strengths. If you have a leader with the gift of vision, then one thing he or she needs is time to meet with other visionaries. A project manager may need specific training and encouragement in detail orientation.

If you look back on your seedbed and your experiences to date, can you recognize what you have received or not received?

Every leader begins somewhere, and that beginning can lead to life or death. Leaders cannot fully come alive until they understand their reality.

The Need for Higher Capacity

The current leadership-development norm in America today is focused on the wrong things. Most of the training is built to expand a leader's knowledge about his specialty or desired field.

We've become so focused on the processes of leadership, however, that we've neglected the hearts and souls of our leaders. This becomes obvious just flipping through the promotional materials for leadership seminars that I receive in the daily mail and online:

- How to Train Your Sales Leaders
- How to Engage Customers for Stronger Revenues
- Learn to Manage Your Leaders Through Motivation Incentives

All of these are focused on the end result rather than on the leader. There is nothing inherently wrong with this type of training—we all need to be proficient and capable—but leadership training should focus on inspiring and influencing people to perform at their highest levels while serving a higher purpose.

Leadership ability determines the ultimate level of your effectiveness. The more you grow and expand your leadership skills, the more opportunities you will have to use your gifts and the more influence you will have.

Raising your capacity for influence should be the cornerstone of your leadership development. Fitness training often focuses first on strengthening the core muscles in the stomach and back because their proper support can protect you from debilitating injuries and increase power and blood flow throughout your body. Likewise, leadership training should strengthen your core first. Then you can build upon your core strengths. Too often, leadership training offers generic instruction instead of specific information geared to you, your talents, and your strengths. Generic leadership training does not work. You cannot influence an organization or team unless you follow a more focused pattern.

Far too much of current leadership training does not provide context or methods for practical application. The assumption is that leaders will know how to apply what they learned to the appropriate situation. And yet, as we have discussed, if leaders do not understand the context of their leadership culture and the style of leader they themselves are, these generic leadership principles can simply be irrelevant to their real world of work.

At GiANT, we often hear from our client's employees that their bosses and supervisors are always trying out the latest "flavor of the month" leadership techniques without talking to them about what they really need from management. And too often, business leaders are inconsistent, using command-and-control one day and consensus building the next. These problems are rooted in the fact that leadership begins within. You have to know yourself before you can lead others.

Knowing First

Strong, effective leaders first develop their inner core: the guiding principles and values they believe in and hope to instill in their teams. Once you are confident in who you are and what you believe in, you can more effectively communicate strategies. To know yourself, you must also take a realistic inventory of your strengths, your weaknesses, your style of leadership, and the challenges in your work environment.

Next you have to get to know your team members: *their* strengths and weaknesses and the challenges that *they* face. To be known is to be respected. When people feel respected, they are more open to working together. And if you are a leader of, say, thousands of people, you must do your best to show that you desire to know people. Oftentimes leaders in large companies are viewed as distant because they are.

As I noted above, in order for this process to succeed you have to be honest in your self-appraisal. Most of the problems that we see with leaders stem from the fact that they fail to acknowledge their weaknesses and blind spots—or those of their team members. How about you?

- How well do you know yourself? What do you want? What do you not want? What do you need right now? What are you afraid of losing?

Questions like these are great friends. They can help you learn more about yourself and those you lead.

- Great leaders are self-aware.
- Great leaders can self-manage.
- Great leaders know those they lead.

Knowing yourself inside and out helps you lead with confidence and humility. Once you learn where your weaknesses lie, you can take steps to manage them.

One of my confidants is my corporate chairman, Rich Christman. He is a great man and a great friend. I always know where I am with Rich because he knows himself so well. Every other week, we spend time on the phone asking each other tough business questions. Often, after discussing a strategy or a new initiative, I'll ask, "Rich, am I thinking right?"

Because he is confident of himself and in our relationship, Rich feels free to be candid with me and to ask probing questions that help give me perspective and a deeper understanding of my own thought processes. Rich and I have a trusting relationship. There are very few areas of our lives we have not shared. And because we know each other so well, we can talk candidly about business strategy and growth or change initiatives.

This is how leadership should work. Rich and I are partners, and he is the chairman of our board. He leads. I follow. We don't become distracted by petty politics and power plays.

Good leadership is about building mutually beneficial relationships, and you can't teach relationship building by applying generic principles. Leadership growth is comparable to the maturation process of human beings. In our youth, we typically make foolish mistakes. As we grow older, we learn from those mistakes and begin to understand our capabilities and our limitations. We can then focus on our strengths, minimize our weaknesses, and be more effective. We mature as people, and as leaders, over time and with effort.

We must always remember that good leadership is a vehicle for people to influence for others' best. To do so we must manage ourselves before putting generic principles on the backs of others. It is our responsibility in order to see true leadership come alive.

CHAPTER 4

THE WALL OF SELF-PRESERVATION

Leading is tough. You know it if you have led. Add to this a significant recession and business pressure and you can find yourself getting a bit locked up in fear. When fear takes over, growth slows. This has happened to me and my team over the past few years. Businesses across the country cut budgets, laid off employees, reduced inventories, and cancelled plans. We tried to hold on to our team members because we believed our services would be in need more than ever during and after this storm. Still, our people were concerned about their jobs, as were millions of others nationwide.

Oddly enough, one key employee came to me during the first few weeks of the recession asking for a promotion and a raise. You can imagine the look on my face. He didn't seem to understand that most companies were cutting jobs, not increasing salaries. He never clued in. Instead he kept pushing for more money and a better position. For his efforts, he found himself on the endangered-employees list.

I was aggravated by his actions, but I understood them. His fears had caused this once-valued employee to go into self-protection mode. But his actions nearly caused him to self-destruct. The harder he pushed, the less inclined I was to keep him on the team.

Luckily for him, I didn't respond to my own fears in the same way that he responded to his. I had a great deal to protect too, but all too often I'd seen leaders endanger the future of their companies because they were trying to protect them during short-term crises.

---

*Leaders need to understand that the protective mode
is not a productive mode.*

Leaders need to understand that the protective mode is not a productive mode. Protectiveness rarely produces gain. While you may get what you want short term, the cost to future growth is much greater. When you hunker down, your view is seriously obscured. Business leaders need to see what lies ahead, in the distance, not just what's right in front of them. Executives who focus on self-preservation risk stagnation.

Executives who focus on self-preservation risk stagnation.

When you find yourself on the defensive, the reason is generally that you fear losing something important. Closing the gates and manning the towers to defend the castle against a siege may be necessary for the short term, but it is not a long-term strategy. A constant mode of self-preservation is no way to live your life or to run a business.

Defensive leadership leads only to mediocrity, and being average will not allow you to thrive in this hypercompetitive global economy. I've consulted over the years with scores of CEOs seeking my help in boosting their own performances and those of top individuals and teams within their organizations. Often, mediocrity is the enemy I've been summoned to dispatch. Now and then, the CEO will candidly admit that he too has lost his way and is dissatisfied with his own performance.

The common culprit blamed in most of these cases is a lack of drive or cooperative effort. There are books and seminars galore offering formulas and prescriptive advice for motivating oneself and one's team members. Most solutions focus on incentive compensation or carrots and sticks. Rarely is the real enemy identified or the correct solution proposed.

What Keeps Leaders Mediocre?

Mediocrity is self-perpetuating; it restrains a leader's influence. This is no way to live or to lead.

So, what keeps leaders mediocre? To answer that question about others, we need to also ask it of ourselves: what keeps you mediocre as a leader? Or, what could lead you to become mediocre? We need to be self-aware, especially in our leadership abilities. Probing questions help us grow.

Most mediocre leaders have something they are trying to protect. When their desire to safeguard turf or status or power takes priority over the desire to positively influence others for the benefit of the greater good, they plunge into mediocrity.

Another surefire path to mediocrity is to view every business dealing purely as a transaction in which you expect something in return for everything you do. Leaders and individuals who fall into the self-preservation mode often find themselves in a transactional loop. Yet transactions themselves rarely lead to long-term gains of any substance. For the most part, one transaction simply leads to another.

The Transaction Trap

One of the most embarrassing moments in my career occurred when, as a young man trying to establish myself, I left a new job after just three days. I'd taken a sales position in a regional office of a national organization. The organization was a good one, but the goal of my job was to retain members, and the company's methods seemed hard-nosed to me. The strategy was designed to close a sale in fourteen minutes. Don't ask me why they decided on fourteen minutes. Maybe fifteen was taken? My training period was all of three days. Then I was booted out of the nest with orders to build my territory. I'd never liked pushy sales people; now I was one of them.

I had to walk door-to-door in small-town Oklahoma, trying to convince business owners to sign on or stay with the company. It was a purely transactional approach. "Every organization needs us," my manager said. One of the first businesses I visited, with my manager shadowing me, was a bar. There we were: two guys in dark blue suits and dark ties strolling into this beer-soaked joint early in the morning. From the look of the clientele, I feared that we'd wandered into a beer brunch for the Hell's Angels.

My manager had instructed me to introduce myself by whipping out my identification card while giving notice that we were from "a company out of Washington, DC."

This was a bad movie in the making. I had visions of the bikers tossing us into a dumpster. The rough woman bartender gave us a look that was almost as scary as the crude message on her T-shirt. "You want to speak to the owner?" she said. "Hey, boys, these two city boys want to talk to the owner!"

I watched in horror as my manager rolled into his slick spiel, as if he were addressing the Rotary Club and not a hostile bunch of hungover bikers. His surefire fourteen-minute sales pitch was greeted by a two-minute warning. Then we were pitched out the door, more or less. The receptions we received at the local barbershop and emu farm were only slightly less unreceptive.

One day on the job, and I'd learned all I ever wanted to know about transactional marketing and self-preserving leadership. We were never instructed to actually listen to the needs of the people we were pitching. Basically, the goal was to rattle off alarming facts about the economic and the political landscape of the country to sway people to renew their subscription to our services. We were all about meeting quotas, not serving needs.

At the end of each day, we were supposed to call into a regional manager and report how many new "partners" we had signed. I beat my manager's record in the first three hours. Later, I learned that this sale was a setup designed to sell me on the job. Everyone beat the phony record on the first day.

By my third day on this miserable job, my conscience threatened a walkout. I stood on a street corner in another small town and called my dad. I told him that I'd been duped into exactly the sort of job I didn't want.

"Son," he said, "that company is not what you are about. You know it. Now, go find a company or person you admire and give them your best by being true to who you are."

My dad has always been my hero. I resigned that day. Three weeks later, I found a job with an amazing family-run company at which sales weren't about stirring up fear and making quotas. Influence was the model.

Transactional businesses are a trap. They pressure employees to do whatever it takes to "hit the numbers," with little focus on the long-term effect or customer relationships. The demand for short-term gains results in a high burn-out rate and no sense of fulfillment.

Transactional selling was not my cup of tea. I preferred a relational approach, in which the goal is to build a trusting relationship with the customer or client so that you come to understand customers' interests and needs and then can offer them products or services that serve them best. Leaders who aspire to greatness and to having a positive and lasting impact will find the "solution-based" relational model more suited to their goals than the transactional "Let's make a deal" model.

Six-Star Relationships

A few years ago, I had the privilege of spending time with the famed hotelier Horst Schulze, the founder and CEO of the West Paces Hotel Group, which manages exclusive Capella hotels around the world. Prior to joining West Paces, Horst gained fame as the brilliant service-minded leader of the Ritz-Carlton hotel chain.

Horst Schulze has built a stellar career around his relational approach to serving customers. The Ritz-Carlton chain distinguished itself with extraordinary service under his leadership. His goal was to build relationships with guests so that they would return to hotels in the chain whenever they traveled. I became a loyal customer during that period, even before I knew Horst. If I stayed for more than a day or two, I could always count on at least a couple of staff members greeting me by name and knowing what sort of things I liked to eat or enjoyed doing. The Ritz chain set the bar high for its competition during those years.

When I met Horst and learned more about him, I was even more impressed with his leadership. He was born and raised in Germany, and while the stereotype for the "Germanic personality" is that they are more attracted to systems and mechanisms than people, Horst is very warm and personable, not to mention service minded. He came up with the tagline, "Ladies and Gentlemen Serving Ladies and Gentlemen" when he was fifteen years old. This became the motto for the Ritz, crystallizing its relational approach to business.

Horst told me that the Ritz-Carlton chain improved its service and its bottom line by defining six main areas of hotel excellence and focusing intensely on each one. He also conducted a benchmark study of the world's best hotel chains to see how his hotels ranked against the competition. "We made it our goal to beat every one of them in each area," he said.

Schulze is now onto another mission. In 2005 West Paces launched a new hotel concept called Capella Hotels and Resorts, which he hopes to build into a unique six-star hotel chain. There are no rankings that include a sixth star, but Horst says his sixth star is the one focused on customer relationships. "Capella is about heart," he said. "It is about focusing on you, the guest. We want to be connected to the lives of our guests."

Horst Schulze set an industry standard with the Ritz-Carlton, and now he is seeking to take hospitality to the next level with his new venture. You have to admire his dedication and drive to achieve higher and higher levels of customer service in an industry that often seems to want to just rent you a room and then gouge you with extra charges for phone calls, minibar snacks, Internet access, and pool chairs.

Under his guidance, the Ritz-Carlton became a premier-brand hotel chain with a loyal customer base. However, his impact extended beyond his own company, as Horst's example influenced other hotel chains and other industries to adapt similar high standards of quality service.

Great leaders with true influence build relationships by serving the needs of those within their spheres of influence, even as they serve the needs of their businesses. This isn't just a business tactic, it is a lifestyle.

To have true influence, you have to move beyond the transactional approach to life and into the relational.

To have true influence, you have to move beyond the transactional approach to life and into the relational. Some people find that more difficult than others. If you feel stuck in the transactional mode, you may feel uncomfortable with the relational model because of insecurities or fears. Your personal self-preservation tendencies may need to be reviewed for you to see real growth in your leadership.

The Reality of Self-Preservation

Think about *self-preservation* for a moment. It is a good word. Our natural instinct is to watch over the things we own, covet, or desire. Each of us protects what is dear to us. These instincts lead us to:

- Lock our doors at night to protect lives and possessions.
- Demand that our kids wear helmets when riding a bike.
- Buckle our seat belts in vehicles.
- Buy insurance.

Your self-preservation and protective instincts are a natural part of your everyday life. Those instincts become a detriment only when they become more important than your growth and fulfillment as a leader and as a person. Self-protection is not the issue. It is *over*protection that is the problem. When you relentlessly hang on to what you've got, you'll never have a hand free to reach for something better. In days of old, self-preservation was expressed on a grand scale by building mighty walls around not only homes but entire communities and nations. When you build walls, you restrict both what goes out and what comes in.

Men and women who build walls to protect their status or income or their sense of security risk also restricting growth in their careers and relationships. They also tend to fall into a very basic transactional approach in which every interaction demands a give and a take. They "do things to get things," but, otherwise, they hide behind the wall.

Great leaders learn to overcome this natural tendency toward self-preservation. They step beyond the walls to give, to serve, and to grow. Great companies do the same, pushing past their protective instincts and seizing new opportunities. Letting go of security and the familiar is not easy. Adam and Eve had to learn self-preservation after being kicked out of the Garden of Eden. It's been in our DNA ever since.

Self-preservation cannot become a lifestyle, not if you want to make a difference in the world. In the end, the walls we build only restrict us. Walls can be built to keep others out, or they can be foundations to build upon. They are not inherently bad; it's the intent of the builder that determines whether the wall is good and useful or whether it is harmful.

The "Protection Wall"

Perhaps the most famous wall of more recent times was the Berlin Wall, which served as a visual demonstration of the ill-willed Soviet Iron Curtain. The Berlin Wall divided Soviet-dominated East Berlin and the liberated and free West Berlin. For almost thirty years, this wall separated families and friends within the same city.

Once walls go up, they are hard to tear down. This is true of cities, countries, and individuals. Walls are built for separating and protecting ownership. Once ownership of a parcel of land is claimed, boundaries are established in the form of fences, property

lines, and walls. Once the borders are built, they can be defended, and most walls have a defensive process to protect them.

In a similar manner, men and women construct inner walls to protect certain aspects of their interior lives. Walls exist within us all. They may be built consciously or unconsciously for our protection, but they can also shut us off from the rest of the world and the opportunities awaiting us there. I can't claim to know what walls you might have erected, but in most cases, the reason we put them up is for self-preservation.

WALLED OFF

The wall of self-preservation is tall and thick. It may protect us even as it offends others. Like most walls, yours and mine require considerable maintenance, and the time we devote to self-preservation might be better spent reaching out and extending our influence. My career is devoted to helping leaders perform at peak levels to have a positive impact. Time after time, the major impediment to peak performance is self-preservation.

The more you labor to guard your status, your reputation, your status quo, the less influence you have on others and in the business world. The less influence you have, the smaller your impact. The reason for this is that influence is based on trust. People do not follow those who are out only to advance their own interests. The more you go into protective mode and withdraw from the people around you, the less they will trust you. It is nearly impossible to trust someone who thinks first and foremost about himself. And the less people trust you, the less influence you will have with them.

Fear, worry, envy, and insecurity dog us all from time to time, if not all the time. But if these feelings are not properly managed, they will force you into a self-imposed solitary confinement, a fortress of your own making, that will only isolate you and hamper your ability to make a mark.

People with a short reach and small strides rarely gain much ground or travel far. You can't give if you are on guard. To have influence, you have to reach beyond your walls and give of yourself for the benefit of others.

DISCOVERING YOUR WALLS

Can you identify the walls of self-preservation that you've constructed? Do you see how these walls may be hindering, not helping you?

My own self-preservation walls were built in childhood, mostly. I was an only child who yearned to be accepted by others, to make connections. I tended to do whatever it took to gain these friendships. I realized that if I made people laugh, we shared an instant connection. So I would use humor as a wall to protect myself from a fear of rejection or from the fear of getting too close to people. If you read about comedians, most of them have built strong walls of protection through humor.

My influence was small because I focused my efforts on gaining approval, acceptance, and confidence from others instead of simply getting to know them. My decisions were based on approval, not on impact. My view was nearsighted. My influence was limited.

It was in my early twenties when I began to understand how I was wired—and walled off. Only then did I begin to acknowledge the gifts I possessed and the value that I could bring to the world. Through the mentoring of some great leaders and upon gaining a better grasp of influence, I began dismantling my walls of self-preservation. I began focusing on others and using humor appropriately, not in self-defense, which has made me a much more well-rounded person.

The Self-Preservation Balance

Self-preservation has its good points. That particular instinct is one reason the human race is still walking this earth. But we are also here because our ancestors evolved from hunters and gatherers to nation builders, inventors, innovators, and entrepreneurs. To evolve, you occasionally have to let go of the old and reach for the new. To lead in the modern world, you have to focus on what the world wants and needs instead of what makes you comfortable.

To lead in the modern world, you have to focus on what the world wants and needs instead of what makes you comfortable.

Let's look in greater depth at how a focus on self-preservation can be detrimental to your growth and fulfillment as a leader and as an individual.

Can you relate to any of these examples of excessive self-preservation?

- CEO: The corporate CEO who is pressured by his board and Wall Street to hit his or her quarterly earnings. With prestige and financial incentives on the line, some CEO's are compelled to do things they would not normally do to hit the numbers. Yet personal relationships suffer because of the extreme focus on business matters. He or she has been so consumed by the pressure to produce that he or she loses track of what is truly important.
- Business Owner: A business owner who once had gone bankrupt told me that he would never again let financial failure happen to him. His self-preservation efforts included creating a financial buffer of cash and savings. He became so fixated on protecting his money that he micromanaged all of his team members and developed a terrible temper as well as nervous tics. Money controlled his mind-set and produced a stifling, overcautious environment that stunted the company's growth.
- Company or Organization: Any company that faces a public relations problem and then tries to cover it up without taking responsibility is in over-the-top self-preservation mode. It seems like these situations come up every month. BP, the British oil giant, tried to downplay the severity of its disastrous 2010 oil spill, especially in its early days, in the Gulf of

Mexico. The perception that the company was being less than truthful had a huge detrimental impact on BP's corporate image and its profits.

- The New, Young Leader: I have had the privilege of hiring and mentoring dozens of great, young leaders. Self-preservation for the young leaders typically begins with overselling themselves to the boss or the team. Typically, these leaders are fixated on major transactional deals that "prove" their worth and showcase their talents. If they don't rein in their ambition, they may simply burn out quickly or wear out their welcome.

- Director/Vice President No. 1: An overemphasis on self-preservation is a predictable problem for people in this position. Envy and the desire for power and status drive many upper-tier executives to manipulate, coerce, and slander in their mad rush to the highest level. Those who find themselves skipped over often express amazement that they weren't chosen. They seem to be unaware that their blind ambition is all too obvious to others.

- Director/Vice President No. 2: A less predictable and more subtle self-preservation tactic is the bunker mentality. Once certain executives reach a comfortable salary and level of authority, they build a (figurative) bunker that is impossible to penetrate. Every move is designed to protect selfish interests. The Detroit automakers were stagnant and near self-destruction for many years because they had so many management types hunkered in their bunkers. They stifle company innovation and growth.

- Employee: It is common for new employees to be focused on their own rewards and achievements. Yet I believe the unbridled search for status, perks, and the pursuit of recognition distracts many new employees from their assigned goals and responsibilities.

- Mother: Do you know a mother consumed with concerns about family finances? Self-preservation drives her to skimp on necessities and put stress on relationships with her children and spouse. Being penny-wise is a good strategy, but when money becomes the primary focus, it can cause more harm than good.

- Father: I have found that when the pressure of job performance wears them down, many dads simply want peace. Fathers often self-preserve by retreating at home. They limit their influence because of this and risk missing out on great opportunities with their children. Many kids grow up feeling like they never knew their father because work pressures led him to seek solitude at home.

- Political Leader: I recently talked with a biographer who stated that interviewing most modern political leaders is a waste of time because their intense tendencies toward self-preservation have turned them into automatons reciting rote speeches instead of answering questions or being authentic.

- Pastor/Civic Leader: The pressure of holding municipal office or church leadership positions can be immense, with so many people to please and limited resources. These service positions can send leaders into self-preservation mode, which generally means that they are able to please few and very little is accomplished. Dynamic church and civic leaders rise above those pressures by doing what is right and ignoring the naysayers.

To be a leader who leaves a lasting legacy and has a positive impact on the lives others, you can't afford to make self-preservation your first priority. We come into the world with nothing, and we leave with nothing. What we have to give is much more important than what we hope to gain.

An overemphasis on self-preservation leads to fear of change, and in a dynamic world, if you and your business don't adapt and adjust when change is required, you will find yourself buried by new technologies, intense competition, and shifting markets.

After many years of observing and serving leaders, I have found that they seem to build walls and go into self-preservation mode to protect the same basic things. While not all-inclusive, the following have come up often in my consulting sessions with top executives:

- Authority—Many men, especially, struggle with this, particularly if they are founders or have run companies for a long time. Authority is the right to use power over other people. It is addictive, and many leaders live in daily fear of losing it.
- Money/Salary—Whether stock, commissions, or salary, money is consistently something that leaders find themselves consumed with and focused upon, often to the detriment of their performances at work and in relationships.
- Time—This most precious commodity is something that leaders have to guard carefully, but too often they overdo it and cram every minute of the day with work without setting aside time for relaxation and relationships.
- Reputation—Protecting your reputation is essential, but the best way to do that is to keep building upon it by being a dy-

namic leader and agent for change. If you spend all of your time guarding your reputation, it's likely people will notice and be guarded themselves.

- Status—Many leaders become enamored with the status that their positions bring them. The danger is that if they lose the job, they will lose their sense of self-worth. The only truly important status is how we rank with our loved ones and our God.

- Perks—Too often, little things take on major importance in the lives of leaders who see perks as their right. Private jets, limousines, vacation retreats—these may have their place, but they should be the rewards, not the goal.

- Energy—The leader who demands to be left alone because he needs to rest might as well paint a target on his back. This form of self-preservation is highly dangerous in a competitive global market. If you take the job, you should be prepared to handle it physically and mentally.

- Family—We naturally desire to protect our families for their safety and for their benefit, but if you overdo it, you'll isolate them and leave them unprepared for dealing with the real world. Again, private schools, gated communities, and security teams certainly have their place, but leaders need to be careful that they don't become so protective that they wall their loved ones off from the world and all that is good about life.

Each of these self-preservation categories revolves around the fear of losing something valuable or failing in front of others. Fear changes behavior.

So, let me ask you what it is that *you* are trying to protect or preserve.

- Your authority?
- Your commissions?
- Your salary?
- Your job?
- Your reputation?
- Your self-esteem?
- Your benefits?
- The perks that come with your title?

Whatever the answer or combination of answers, you should understand that poor performance is often traced to a person's efforts to preserve or protect the status quo. These two *P*s, protection and preservation, can mire a career and a life in mediocrity. Self-preservation is the chief "capacity constraint" of individuals who feel "stuck."

When leaders feel compelled to circle the wagons, they often tend to lose more than they gain. Here are the primary reasons for this. When you are a leader focused only on self-preservation . . .

- You become more focused on you than on others. This leads only to people being put off by you, as they see you self-centered and insecure. They know you are detached, and that leads to a lack of trust, which prevents effective leadership.
- You become defensive. Have you ever seen a hawk protect its nest? You may just be walking by the tree, but the bird sees you as a threat and attacks. Leaders focused on self-preservation

act in a similar manner. They see everyone as a threat, which, again, renders them incapable of positive influence.

- Your performance deteriorates. As someone focuses more on himself, he takes his eyes off of what is really important. Once again, what he hopes doesn't happen begins to happen. The quality of the person's work decreases as his focus on himself increases.

A total focus on self-preservation can destroy your career as a leader and ruin relationships because you isolate yourself and push others away. When in self-preservation mode, you may feel that you are only protecting what you value most, but too often your actions are self-defeating, and you wind up losing the things that you value the most. The negative ramifications of intense self-preservation are obvious to those around you, but your view becomes myopic.

I've experienced this loss of perspective in my own career. For a time, I was so absorbed in turning around one of our companies that I developed tunnel vision. Fear of failure overwhelmed me, affecting my day-to-day interactions with partners, employees, and stockholders. Later, when I reflected on that period, I realized that my fear was like a virus, infecting everything I did and dramatically altering the way that I related to others. You know what sticks with me from that time? I remember a sensation—almost like a *smell*—of overpowering fear and anxiety.

You've probably observed coworkers or bosses whose careers hit a rough spot, and they seemed to be in a downward spiral, losing their tempers, making bad decisions, acting out of character. The salesman who is afraid of losing commissions puts intense pressure on his customers. The friend who is feeling insecure becomes overly needy.

Years ago, I consulted with a leader who was consumed with preserving his lifestyle. He had built a company to a modest level of profitability. Yet virtually 100 percent of his profits went to maintaining his over-the-top lifestyle. Expenditures for his wardrobe, mortgage, cars, and exclusive vacations drained his finances. Instead of investing in new technologies that would grow his company, he spent it on himself. He could not see it at the time, but he was preserving himself into financial ruin. He could have tripled the money he spent on his extravagant lifestyle if he had invested it in the growth of his company.

He resisted my efforts to convince him to corral his personal spending. As a result, his company fell behind its competition. He's had to cut his payroll and his team just to survive. His focus on short-term extravagance has crippled the business he created and threatened its future.

This might seem like an extreme case of self-absorption, but I see it everywhere. To have true influence, you can't simply focus on yourself and your needs. You may even have to take risks that force you to ignore self-preservation for the greater good. That is not an easy decision to make. You have to make a living, pay the bills, and feed your family, after all. Your natural instinct tells you to collect, preserve, and guard. But left unchecked, your self-preservation instincts can cause you to self-destruct.

Threads of Self-Preservation

If you find yourself going into an extreme level of self-protection that isolates you and hinders your ability to be an effective leader, the first step is to look at the source of the fear that is driving your actions. Think of it as following a thread that has unraveled from the fabric of your character. You are the product of your genetic makeup, your upbringing, your environment and your relationships. The patterns of our lives are built from these strands. When one is damaged or torn, it threatens the integrity of the whole.

The thread of DNA and personality shapes our way of thinking and communicating, which affects our preservation tendencies. For instance, introverts tend to guard time more than extroverts, as time alone helps them to recharge more than being with people. Deep thinkers may self-preserve tasks more than those more guided by emotions because facts are easier to process than emotions.

The thread of upbringing shapes our view of the future. If you grew up in an affluent family with virtually unlimited means, that can affect your feelings about self-preservation. We may be more likely to be swayed by image and reputation based on the peer pressure of family and society. Often we adopt the same approach practiced by our parents. What they valued, we value. What did your parents hold dear and strive to preserve? This may give you insight into your own tendencies.

The thread of work experience may cause you to lean in one direction or another. You may find yourself trying to avoid a particular work situation that hampered your career in the past, without realizing that the circumstances are different in this case. If you once worked for an undercapitalized venture, for example, you may be overcautious about taking on company debt even in a more stable company.

The thread of relationships affects the way we deal with everyone around us. Childhood abuse often leaves the victim fearful of intimacy and unwilling to trust others. A broken partnership or marriage can leave people afraid to enter into another relationship.

The thread of faith typically leads to a more balanced view of self-preservation, but if someone's faith is diminished by a betrayal or a tragedy, a life can unravel quickly.

Each thread of your character affects your life as a leader. We are what we have been born into, experienced, and seen. That is how self-preservation occurs. You may see this more clearly in your own life by reflecting on the following questions:

- What challenges did your mom and dad go through in their lives, from birth to adulthood?
- What are you naturally good at? What are your weaknesses?
- Was there any abuse or negative influences in your childhood by an adult?
- What were your earliest jobs, from your teenage years through your twenties? Think about the positives and negatives of these positions. What impact did those work experiences have on your approach to your career?
- What is your current family situation? Think of the positives and negatives.
- Can you list your greatest fears?
- Who do others see you to be? Who do you see yourself to be?
- What is your dream? Is it within reach?
- Do you currently feel grounded? Stuck? Out of balance? Out of control?

To be a positive influence and a leader worth following, you must deal with your own insecurities and fears before you can empower others. To do this, you might have to deal with memories and issues that are unpleasant and disconcerting, maybe even painful.

From time to time, I've conducted assessments of my own career. I've seen how I allowed challenges with recessions, partnerships, clients, and employees to alter my perspective. I've had to deal with my weaknesses and leverage my strengths.

Real Leadership

Tom was the CEO of his family's manufacturing company, located in a small town. He led the business well for years, receiving accolades and awards for innovation and corporate values. His success was well earned.

Despite his accomplishments, Tom is a humble person. He has sailed around the world, lived overseas, explored amazing sights, and he has a great family. Yet he never boasts of his accomplishments, nor does he hog the credit for his business success. He also uses the profits from his business to help others. Tom has given away large sums of money to charity but he has also given of himself. He has been a positive influence upon many people, including me.

Over the last five years I've learned a great deal from talking with him, but even more from observing how he treats other people. For example, for more than ten years, Tom has been helping a troubled alcoholic, a man who has driven off nearly everyone else in his life because of his thirty-year addiction. The alcoholic was once a wealthy man with a large trust fund that he depleted. He would have been homeless and unable to care for himself if Tom hadn't stepped in. What is most remarkable is that the alcoholic hasn't always shown appreciation. Because of the man's poor reputation in the small community, others have disparaged Tom for helping him, but my friend has continued to do what he feels is right.

Obviously, Tom doesn't place a high priority on self-preservation. When I asked him about his service and loyalty to this difficult man, he offered this reply: "God has given me patience for this unlovable guy. I asked God for help loving the unlovable, and He made it happen for me. Helping this guy has changed the way I view everyone."

Tom is a role model as a business leader and as a person. For him, it's not about taking credit or acquiring material things. He is unselfish, loyal, and generous.

True influence is possible when you hold true to your principles and values and when you use your God-given gifts for the benefit of those around you. If you find that difficult in your work and relationships, then you need to break through whatever is keeping you from serving others as a positive influence.

CHAPTER 5

FOR ME, AGAINST ME, OR FOR YOURSELF?

Whether you acknowledge it or not, you have an agenda. If that statement makes you defensive, let me assure you: I have an agenda too. We all do.

An agenda, in its simplest terms, is an "intent in action." This is why we tend to be fearful of one leader's agenda, while welcoming the agenda of another.

To have an agenda indicates that you are alive and dynamic. The nature of your agenda can be either benevolent or malevolent.

- An agenda is the organized action of intent.
- Intent is the purpose or desire.
- Action is carried out to implement intent.
- Motive is the intended outcome.

To understand leadership in light of influence, we must understand motive and the threads of intent. Every leader has a motive for taking actions. Every leader has intentions. The question is, What is the desired outflow of those intentions?

Since we all have motives, your day-to-day decisions are based on what you like to do and don't like to do, and what you ultimately want. For instance, I don't like running errands. I abhor stopping what I am doing (or planning to do) to get into a car and drive somewhere, only to wait in line. That is a nightmare for me. Why? Because the errand usually doesn't fit into my agenda or match up to my organized intent. I know in running errands that I can't control the stoplights or the checkout lines or the crowds. It is simply a nuisance preventing me from doing what I aspire to do. Therefore, errands are rarely on my Saturday agenda. My wife and children, however, often have their own plans for my agenda.

Motive and intent drive agendas, yet there is rarely much contemplation or discussion of those core drivers. Spend thirty minutes listening to a political talk show or the top-of-the-hour news and you will hear phrases such as: "The president passed a sweeping reform today, which has been on the top of his agenda." Or, "It is evident that this divisive move was not on the president's agenda."

Agendas are a real part of our everyday leadership world, and they reveal our intent. Motives reflect the heart and inspire action. Motives reflect your desired end goals. Intent is the catalyst fostered from within that leads to decisions and actions that determine the course of your life. When your intent becomes organized, in an action-oriented way, it becomes your agenda.

This is precisely why influence is so important. Negatively inspired agendas typically kill long-term leadership cultures, whereas clear influence motives help leadership come alive. Knowing your agenda is the first step to understanding your personal leadership.

Knowing Your Agenda

It has been said that you can easily understand your priorities by analyzing where you spent your money and who you called within a recent period of time; say, a month or so.

The same is true with your agenda. A quick review of your journal or to-do list over the past month will reveal your agenda and the intentions that drive your decisions and actions each day. Would you be willing to share that information with your teammates?

Do you know your agenda? Have you analyzed your real intent? I believe that the best leaders are those who challenge themselves. True influencers desire to be the best so that they can bring out the best in others. They self-assess, monitoring their own motives and actions to ensure that they stay within their core values and principles. Those leaders who do not honestly monitor and assess themselves may end up in the same dark place as onetime investment guru Bernie Madoff.

You should begin your business and your leadership career with a much better end in mind. In 2002 Matthew Myers and I started the GiANT companies. Our first business was called GiANT Partners. This business focuses on growing companies by helping the CEO and his leadership team implement growth strategies. In our initial meeting, we explored our own motives for launching the business. In fact, Matthew is the most dedicated motive checker I know. He is gifted in asking the right questions to challenge the intent of every strategy or business decision.

Both of us had substantial business experience, including successes and some failures too. We were pleased to discover that we shared similar motives with this new endeavor. Here is a list of those initial desires and motives:

- We wanted to help leaders change for the better—to grow both personally and professionally.
- We didn't want to manage a lot of people, at least for the first few years.
- We wanted freedom—both financial independence and personal time.
- We wanted a creative outlet for our business skills, and we hoped to have a positive impact on leaders within the community.
- We hoped to change the world one leader at a time.

Once we'd agreed upon our agenda, we were off and running. I can honestly say that most of our intentions have held up. We continue to check in with each other about our intentions, and we've given each other permission to prod our partner if necessary. Great partnerships work because of that sort of trust.

Our intentions helped us to form our strategy, which has benefited all of our GiANT enterprises to this day. This agenda took our company down a certain path because the way we structured the company was dictated by our strategy—the same strategy born of our intent and motives.

It is important to note that often a leader's agenda changes over time and due to circumstance. Intent can change. Motives can be altered. You see it often in men and women who have undergone a significant life change, through pain or gain. What they once wanted, they no longer desire. New motives overtake past intent. New seasons affect a leader's agenda.

So, what is your agenda? What is your intent?

An easy exercise to help you process your intent is to answer the following questions:

- What do you hope happens in your work?
- What do you not want to happen?
- What do you expect is going to happen?
- What are you afraid of losing?
- What are you trying to prove? To whom?
- What are trying to hide? From whom?

These are motive-busting questions. They pull intent out into the light. Those who desire to become a true influence will love these questions, as facing the answers will make them better leaders.

The Attributes of a True Influence Leader

It may be helpful to share a list of attributes that I have accumulated over the years that define a true influence leader—a leader that has come fully alive. He or she

- leads with vision;
- leads from the head and the heart;
- practices humility and service to others (lets go of status and self-preservation);
- influences rather than pushes or demands;
- invests in the success of others first;
- rises above unethical practices, pressure, and petty politics;
- attracts a diverse and dedicated team of future leaders;
- delivers more than expected (loaves and fishes);
- wields the tools of forgiveness, gratitude, and laughter;
- reaches out to make the last first.

The above list can occur within each of us if—and only if—we are willing to examine the inner core of motive and overcome our own fears, pressures, and selfish tendencies.

Some of you may be asking why this doesn't happen more often. Why don't more leaders exhibit the ten attributes above? We will address that question throughout the book, and I will ask the same about you as well. The answer lies in your motive for influence.

Leadership is influence. Influence is power.
How that power is used comes from the intent of the leader,
from the motives of the heart.

Leadership is influence. Influence is power. How that power is used comes from the intent of the leader, from the motives of the heart.

Here is an easy way to measure the depth of your influence. Your team, your family, or your friends are asking a question, "Is he or she for me, against me, or for themselves?"

The answer to this question will show your influence within your organization or group.

Think about it this way: people around you are either for you, against you, or just for themselves. While there may be variations on these three motives, this concept generally holds true. Reality television shows are perfect examples of intent. In most cases, there will be a small group of people who will try to manipulate others to wear them down and eventually force them out of the game. In each episode, you can determine who is for whom and against whom. It is a fascinating and often disconcerting look at humanity.

Take out a sheet of paper and make a short list of people in your life (business, home, family, and so forth). Answer this question for each: "Is this person for me, against me, or for himself/herself?"

Revealing isn't it? Now turn the tide. What would they say you were to them? For them, against them, or for yourself?

The reality is that the majority of people are self-centered. Rarely are people against you. It's more that they are for themselves and totally driven by self-interest. It's human nature. Most people I know are in survival mode day to day, doing whatever they can to take care of their families and their businesses and organizations. I fall into that mode, and it's likely that you do too.

What would happen, though, if you intentionally demonstrated that you were *for* the people on your list? You would see amazing changes transpire in the lives of those around you if they knew you were invested in their success as well as your own.

Imagine yourself becoming so significant in other peoples' lives that you are not only memorable but also valuable to them. Imagine people believing that you want the best for them and understanding that you are for them. Imagine that they open up to you, enabling you to wield true influence and have an impact. Imagine experiencing, as a result of these things, the fulfilling relationships you've dreamed of at work and at home.

By "influence," I am suggesting a holistic view. I believe that influence is unleashed before work, during work, and after work, not solely in one part of the day.

A "For Me" Example

Brandon Hutchins, president of Gaskins Surveying and Engineering in Marietta, Georgia, is a great example of being someone who is for me. I have rarely met someone so devoted to encouraging me as Brandon is. He is intentional and pure in his motives. He simply believes in who I am and what I am about. There are many reasons for this. We have spent considerable time working on his business and leadership style. Yet, we have also connected philosophically.

Brandon practices 24/7 influence. He is a leader, at home and at work. Dozens of people observe this daily. Yet Brandon's influence goes much further than the norm. Brandon has decided to give of himself to grow his community too.

He and a number of other influencers have started a movement within Marietta to nurture positive leadership. In a given week, you will find Brandon meeting with leaders and aspiring leaders at breakfast or lunch, working on growing his team within his company, being a great dad to his four kids, and being a great husband to his wife, Nancy.

Brandon is one of the most intentional influencers I have ever met. His desire to influence is a lifestyle, not just a principle. For instance, he is active in serving the leaders in his company in more ways than just work. I have heard dozens of stories where Brandon has encouraged leaders through marriage issues, personal financial struggles, and personal growth.

Brandon is not afraid of challenges or of challenging others. He is a great example of an unsung hero, but he is also a valued commodity: the everyday leader. There are thousands of people like Brandon who are committed to being and doing their best by knowing and leading themselves first, then knowing and leading others to bring out the best in them as well.

Brandon offers an example of the power of influence and an intent of being for others. He is having a huge impact in his community, and that doesn't just happen—no matter how much you desire it. To say that you want to influence others is only the first step. Influential leadership demands hard work. Being for others is hard work, but so very rewarding in many tangible and intangible ways.

To influence others, you must follow a process that is calculated but appears natural. People recognize inauthenticity in those who aspire to lead them. Suspicion and cynicism are at all-time highs thanks to the corrupt leadership that has been so prevalent in recent years. You'll find few people who readily accept that a leader is truly invested in their success in addition to his or her own.

The way to have true and welcomed influence is to begin the journey within.

The Influence Model

Influence is a process. There are no shortcuts for attaining lifelong impact on others. While there are no formulas to influence, I have developed a model to help you in the process.

I created this model almost a decade ago. I had experienced success in influencing other leaders, even some twice my age. I was often approached by others wanting to know how I had developed my leadership style and influenced the number of people that I had at my age. I created a visual response originally scribbled in an old, worn-out Moleskine journal. You are welcome to challenge it or add to it. It was made to explain to others in simple terms.

Influence starts like this: first you must have a hunger to serve others and the willingness to self-assess and self-motivate through the process to maintain healthy, authentic relationships.

Action is the key to this influence model. I have highlighted seven essential actions for exerting true influence in the lives of others. The first three are detailed in this chapter. I will describe the other four later on.

Action No. 1: Give Trust to Become Trustworthy

The first stage of influence is to trust others. It is both the foundation for growth and the bedrock for impact. Without trust there is no influence.

The art of establishing trust is taught by scores of authors and countless training companies. Yet trust is not established merely by applying the right set of tools. Trust is the reward of unwavering character. To trust someone without knowing the person's character is a gamble. Until you know what lies within someone's heart and soul, you should not give your complete trust.

Trust your instincts. If someone makes you feel uneasy upon first impression, do not disregard that gut feeling. Work to learn more of what lies within the person, what principles and virtues guide the individual.

I've heard this initial impression described as the "smell test." If your nose picks up the odor of something burning, you investigate. I'd advise you to be just as responsive to any sense that someone might not be worthy of your trust.

One frequent tip-off in reading the trustworthiness of someone is to look at the company he or she keeps. I subscribe to the old saying "Birds of a feather flock together." Good character connects with good character, and bad character is attracted to bad character.

Relationships are often built on common ground. There's a reason that one of the first questions we ask of a new acquaintance is, "So where are you from?" Shared experience opens the way to shared information and the building of interpersonal chemistry, a binding agent in building trust.

Finding commonality should be an authentic process. Don't go along to get along. Ask tough questions to clarify what people are wanting and needing if you sense they should be asked. Many sales training formulas teach ways to establish common ground through manipulation or false pretenses. That is not what I'm endorsing.

True trust takes time. Sometimes the trust process can be expedited, especially if you have a mutual connection. For instance, most organizations prefer to hire from the referrals of current employees because trust has already been established within the network. The popular business-themed social networking site LinkedIn is based on this same philosophy.

You must be careful with this, though. There are times when you might believe that you have established trust, only to quickly find that you've been reckless or not careful enough in your due diligence.

Several years ago, I met with a CEO who was close with an acquaintance of mine. Because of that shared mutual contact,

I presumed we had already established trust. I hustled in and offered him a grand vision of working together. About twenty minutes into the meeting, I began to realize that I had no actual influence in his life. He was guarded in his trust with me, and he misinterpreted what I'd told him. I was shocked. That had never happened to me before. I knew my intentions were honorable. He did not.

We eventually worked through his distrust issues—which were partly my fault for rushing the relationship and partly his for guarding his interests so zealously. He suspected that I was cozying up to him so that I could make a bid for his company. I was trying to be of service and missed the clues. For a brief period, the budding relationship floundered. The influence model, however, helped me to back up and start over. The model also helped me with my view of the other person.

Ultimately, trust is about character and whether you have the character to be trustworthy. If you do, chemistry between you is more likely to happen. If there is no chemistry, you either have a trust issue or a personality issue. Personality clashes or competence issues can prevent two parties from connecting even though both are good people and trustworthy.

The key is to have an accurate reading of where you stand with the other person. This requires self-awareness and the ability to read interpersonal cues. Good character is also a requirement, and my definition of this goes beyond merely being drug free and honest. I look at a person's whole character. As my friend Dr. Henry Cloud, a clinical psychologist, leadership consultant, and author, writes in his book *Integrity: The Courage to Meet the Demands of Reality*:

The people who possess [competency and the ability to connect with others] are a dime a dozen. There is no shortage of talented, brainy people who are very, very good at what they do and are able to work the system and schmooze other people to get things done. There are zillions of them, and we all see them every day. But if [you] are truly going to make it, [you] have to have the third ingredient as well: [You] have to have the character to not screw it up.

If, like most people, you've been burned by someone or some company that you trusted in the past, you may have trust issues. While most people eventually come to see betrayals as a lesson learned and move on, some have lingering problems that make it difficult for them to be trusting. If that's an issue in your life, you'll have to learn to be both trusting and trustworthy to have true influence as a leader. Harsh memories of broken trust can be an impediment to significant leadership.

If you choose not to trust those who lead you, then you will hold back opinions and miss the opportunity to expand your influence. Your trust issues may even cause you to be perceived as unresponsive and incapable of leading.

I've worked to help leaders who have serious trust issues because of bad experiences. Often they are judged to be untrustworthy by their team members, so these wounds can be a serious handicap unless allowed to heal. I've encountered that situation twice, and in both cases the individuals were so guarded that they had a difficult time influencing others.

Trust is a two-way street. You must give your trust while also proving yourself trustworthy. They go hand in hand. So how do you do that in the real world? Here are some suggestions:

- Realize that it is okay to measure character. This is not judging others but rather common sense to establish the right foundation for a positive connection.
- Find common ground. Much can be built on the foundation of true common connections. It is invaluable to accomplish great things.
- Test character in small things first. It is a fact that more comes when small things have been stewarded well. Do not dismiss the small beginnings of large opportunities.
- Be willing to give people the benefit of the doubt until they prove unworthy. Most people believe that if you are not for me, you are against me. In contrast, I believe that if you are *not against* me, you are *for* me. Change your approach to trust.
- Be open and welcoming. Hellos and good-byes are the most obvious displays of trust. Just like the introduction and closure of a story, so too are the entrances and exits of people.

To present yourself as trustworthy, I suggest the following:

- Learn to give your trust to others. This is hard for most people because they are stuck in the past pain of broken promises. Learning to give takes time and practice, but it is so worth the effort.
- While you are measuring another person's character, be aware that your character is also under scrutiny.
- Be consistent. Whether you say yes or no, stick to it. Make it clear what you want or don't want, so that there is no room

for dangerous ambiguity. I continue to learn this one the hard way, as I tend to be so people focused.

Trust is the first stage of influence. We must seek to trust others as we ourselves become trustworthy. It is an action word and something that must be actively pursued.

Action No. 2: Become Credible, Not Just Smart

The second action point closely follows the first. Trust is about our character, but it is affected by our competencies. To have one without the other isn't enough. In fact, depending on the relationship, others may check out your credibility before they examine your character.

Credibility typically comes with high levels of competency and depth of knowledge. The desire for credibility is usually coupled with a "prove it" mentality, because skepticism and cynicism are at such high levels. You can claim competence, but words are not enough. You'll have to prove yourself to establish credibility.

The search to become credible starts at a young age. For three years, my kids were in an international public school with over forty countries represented. It was ranked number one in the state for academics. Chess and music seemed to be the school sports. Each afternoon many of the kids from other countries would go directly from school to a tutor for even more instruction.

You can imagine how we felt as we sent our kids off to the creek to play or to the backyard for a rousing round of kickball. When we asked some of the other parents why they put their kids through such a regimen, they told us that it was because of competitive pressure they felt as immigrants or visitors in the United States. They felt that high grades, special tutoring, and advanced classes gave their children a leg up. Their cultures value competence, and they were doing their best to see that their children were high achievers.

This happens in the business world as well, as students flood into MBA programs to enhance their resumes. Credentials suggest credibility. Students seeking an edge are often obsessed with earning advanced degrees at prestigious universities. The sort of credibility I'm referring to goes deeper.

Credibility comes when you put your competencies to work in service to others so that your knowledge and skills make a difference—which in turn makes you relevant.

To be a true influence, you need to be credible, not simply "smart." Credibility comes when you put your competencies to work in service to others so that your knowledge and skills make a difference—which in turn makes you relevant. I know many smart people who lack relevance and, thus, credibility. Smart people who don't use their gifts to make a positive impact risk becoming irrelevant.

The power of competence is unleashed when a person effectively wields knowledge and skills and achieves relevance. These competent people become credible, which moves them closer to true influence.

Bond Payne is chairman of Heritage Trust, a trust bank headquartered in Oklahoma City. The company was created to serve families and individuals with highly competent investment performance and financial stewardship. When you meet Bond, you automatically get the sense that he knows what he is doing. Bond is one of the most competent leaders I know. He and his team have developed the right combination of highly competent advisors who are relationship-first people. It is no wonder Heritage Trust continue to grow: clients simply like them and trust them. And they should.

Bond understands the intentionality needed to create a culture that exudes this combination of trust and credibility. They must go hand in hand. He understands this because he longs for it himself in others. I believe it is Bond's hunger for influence and proper leadership that drives him to create it himself.

Trust is crucial. Credibility is vital. These are the first stages of influence. Influence begins with this combination of developed character and relevant competence. Every organization longs for trustworthy employees who are credible.

Action No. 3: Be Intentional In Your Influence

To influence is a mixture of purposeful action and virtuous character. It is a lifestyle—an intentional lifestyle. To be intentional means to take conscious action and follow through with what you have intended to do. The virtue of intentional action is obvious. You probably wouldn't be inclined to pick up a book entitled *Accidental Parenting* or *Unintentional Leadership*. Endearing? I think not. You can't expect children to raise themselves or businesses and organizations to find their own way. Action is required. Purposeful and intentional action is the only way to produce the results you want for your life and your career.

Companies need to raise their capacities, build growth infrastructures, and empower leaders who will take them to the next level of success. The only leaders who can do that are selfless leaders with good character and relevant credibility.

An Intentional Influence Culture

Chris Carneal, the founder and president of Atlanta-based Booster Enterprises, combines high character and trustworthiness with competence and credibility. Booster is the parent company for several brands focused on leadership development for students under the age of twenty-five. Its core business is Boosterthon Fun Run, which serves over three hundred thousand kids and thirty thousand teachers and administrators in eighteen states. Boosterthon raises funds for schools through a week of health and fitness; it also teaches leadership development to children ages six to twelve. With more than one hundred twentysomething employees, these leaders are role models for every school student.

Chris created Booster Enterprises while he was a student at Samford University in Birmingham, Alabama. He recognized the need for a student-led, values-centered, fitness-based method for schools to raise funds. Character education is at the heart of everything the company does.

Influence is the centerpiece of its business model. Boosterthon's motto is "CTW," which stands for "Change the World," and they devote themselves to accomplishing this every day by becoming the best leaders possible by being accountable to each other and by being willing to learn in reading, relationships, and experience.

I admire Booster Enterprises because:

- It has a clearly defined mission and vision.
- It hires people who fit that mission. It takes months to get into the Booster system because of its hiring focus.
- It invests in itself first. Each new Booster teammate works through a twelve-month introductory process.
- The company realizes that you cannot give what you don't

possess, so it holds one another accountable to grow as leaders.

- It maintains goal charts, and the team members meet regularly with one another. In fact, all new leaders are given cards to review every day to assess their roles and how they affect the team as a whole. They also must note five things that they will do each day to be successful with the entire team and the customer.
- Each area leader is responsible for grooming his or her own replacement.

In essence, Boosterthon Fun Run has built a leadership culture that fosters influence on one another internally, which leads to a positive impact externally. This tone is set by Chris in his routines, personal notes, and intentional one-on-one time with his key leaders. He leads by example and has learned to influence by creating a culture of following one another's positive leadership style.

The combination of character and high competence leads to the outflow of trust and credibility.

Every leader can influence. Every organization can structure itself to develop a culture of influence. The combination of character and high competence leads to the outflow of trust and credibility. To be like Chris, Booster Enterprises, and other truly influential companies, it is vital to intentionally wield your knowledge and skills to positive effect.

That is why living with conscious intent is so very important. The more intentional and confident you are as a leader, the more effective you will be. When people know you are for them, their demeanor and relational skills change for the better. It is uncertainty that stalls growth and hinders progress.

Jo Kirchner, CEO of Primrose Schools, a preschool franchise based in Acworth, Georgia, is another model for living with conscious intent. Jo is responsible for leading Primrose Schools, managing its vision, brand, and business strategies. With the founders of the company, she helped launch the concept of franchising a premier educational environment for preschool children. Since then, Primrose has grown from 4 schools in Atlanta to more than 212 schools in fifteen states. It is recognized as one of the top entrepreneurial enterprises in the country.

With all of her success, the very first thing I noticed about Jo was that she was genuinely interested in me and what I had to say. I have found that Jo has a consistent spirit of authenticity. Many people feel the same way. They inevitably know that she is for them, and it has to do with who she is and how she views others. She seems to have done a masterful job of building trust and credibility in order to influence others for their benefit. That is true success.

One of the keys to intentional influence is to let people know you are truly engaged with them through your tone of voice, inflections, and body language, but also through tangible action on their behalf. Some people are better at being intentional socially than others. Some need to plan intentionality more than others. No matter what your personality type, though, you can't expect others to trust you and to buy into you until you prove yourself trustworthy by buying into them.

Responsive Influence

My friend who is a lieutenant general in the US Army says the army gives men and women rank, but it is a rank to serve others and their families. He added that the army promotes those leaders who handle power well and whether they act out of self-preservation or selflessness. The army officer tells his young men and women, "Be the type of leader you want to follow."

The military leader told me that he looks for officer candidates who have "integrity and selfless leadership." He looks for soldiers whose word is their bond. He needs officers with less of "it's about me."

The lieutenant general requires obedience of his men, but it isn't blind obedience. His men understand that obeying orders is critical to the success and survival of the entire unit.

To understand influence is to understand responsiveness. To be responsive is to be aware of others first, especially as you lead them. The desire to keep improving and increasing the value of your gifts reflects an attitude of receptiveness. The young soldier who leads with humility and serves his men offers another example.

To be responsive is to handle authority and influence as a stewardship, not a divine right. When you are responsive, you gain even more respect for the way you handle your influence. You have a choice. Those who choose not to be responsive to their team members often pay a price.

Think about those currently around you who are not responsive to you or others in your organization. They simply paint themselves in a corner by their own belligerence. In most cases, people celebrate their departure.

This extends to our government. The congressional elections of 2008 and 2010 specifically highlighted the consequences of an unresponsive Congress that diminished and ignored the will of the people who voted for them in the first place. And so, an overwhelming majority swept out congressional leaders who were perceived to be defiantly focused on their own agenda rather than the agenda of the people they were elected to serve.

Influence is a process. To truly impact others, it is vital to understand the connection between character and competence. Being for others is an attitude and a strategy. It can be learned and taught, but it must be intentional in a leader's life in order for leadership to come alive within an organization.

Leadership comes alive when you are willing to lead yourself first and then others.

CHAPTER 6

THE BREAKTHROUGH

Breakthroughs are cause for celebration:

- The student who finally masters algebra.
- The company that hits record numbers.
- The individual who overcomes an addiction.
- The country that deposes a dictator.

Lives are changed, organizations succeed, and people thrive through breakthroughs. But it takes hard work to break through any wall. You must desperately desire what is on the other side. Of course, you have to see it to want it. Too often, leaders lack vision. They can't break through because they are blind to the opportunities and possibilities.

What is on the other side? If I tell you, will you seek it? I hope so—for your own sake and for the sake of those who follow you. Remember: we don't simply need more leaders, we need dynamic, positive, world-changing leaders—true influencers. These are the leaders who can awaken leadership again in this country and throughout our world.

If you are willing to break through, you will find greater fulfillment than you've ever known. Your relationships will be richer. Opportunities will abound. If you are willing to be a true influencer, the rewards will be significant and memorable.

A Breakthrough Perspective

Chris, a longtime friend, has been the CEO of several large organizations. He is well known in venture capital circles around the world and has been successful in turning around global companies. My friend, who is a native of Scotland, has had amazing experiences, but he is now looking at the next phase of his life. He said he is considering two distinct paths. One would allow him to share his knowledge as a mentor to younger business leaders, to help them pursue their dreams. The other path would be to focus on new business opportunities for himself.

When Chris talks about working with younger entrepreneurs, his eyes light up with passion and enthusiasm. Yet he told me that some of his colleagues have chided him for considering that path. They say that he should keep his options open for his own new ventures instead of investing in the success of others.

As we discussed his options, Chris talked with admiration about his eighty-two-year-old father, who was living on the coast of Scotland and seemed completely fulfilled. For more than sixty years, his father ran a school for juvenile delinquents. He gave of himself as a true influence to these boys, many of whom had never had someone invest in their success. Chris said his father's former students often come to see him, to thank him for being a positive influence on their lives.

After reflecting on his father's life, Chris had a breakthrough. He saw the life that he wanted—a life of fulfillment from helping others— and I imagine he will have no problem deciding which path to take.

Self-Pursuit Versus Self-Fulfillment

My friend's story illustrates the conflict within many leaders torn between pursuing their own rewards or helping others achieve their goals. Let's examine each pathway so that we can fully understand this concept.

- Self-pursuit is the effort to attain or secure things for ourselves. This is a self-absorbed effort to obtain things that make us look better in the eyes of others or the pursuit of selfish desires to feel better.
- Self-pursuit rarely leads people to become content. In fact, the paradox is that the most discontented people I know are those who work the hardest at pursuing things they think will bring them pleasure. The truth is that striving for "things" to fulfill you only creates a longing for more.
- Self-fulfillment is the state of being complete. To be fulfilled is to be both content and full. It has less to do with selfish pursuit and more to do with contentment.
- Self-fulfillment comes from within—not from material things or outside approval but from a centered sense of authenticity and self-acceptance. Fulfillment is like being in your favorite restaurant, with your favorite people, ordering your favorite

meal. At the end of the meal, you are fulfilled and want nothing more than to savor the experience.

Do you see the difference?

Many leaders work night and day in pursuit of things they hope will fulfill them. Things such as money, status, power, cars, houses, etc. Yet these things, once attained, rarely do so. There are also those leaders who work to help others grow and flourish. Those leaders are far more likely to be fulfilled. They are secure, authentic, and fulfilled to be a positive influence. I can name dozens of leaders who are fulfilled in what they do every day. They've chosen to focus on serving others. They've broken through.

Dr. David Wright is a clear and perfect example of this. Dr. Wright is provost at Indiana Wesleyan University. IWU is renowned for its exponential growth as a university and for its strong online programs. Dr. Wright, one of the most brilliant, humble leaders, is a reason for this success. His strengths have positioned this small Midwestern private liberal arts school into a regional powerhouse with international acclaim. Dr. Wright gets it. He gets that it isn't about him. He has overcome his own self-pursuits to be a part of something bigger than himself. His style of leadership empowers people to think bigger, which is precisely what has happened for a small Indiana school—it thinks bigger than most. When you give up yourself to be a part of something bigger than yourself, you get to be a part of something big.

Action No. 4: Break Through Your Walls of Self-Preservation

The influence model calls upon leaders to abandon a model of self-preservation for one of service. Here are some practical ways to influence others:

- Counseling a good friend through a deep depression and into recovery and a much better life.
- Listening to an entrepreneur's excitement over a plan that will improve both his business and his personal relationships.
- Helping an influential nonprofit company reorganize to be twice as efficient and effective to those it serves.

To realize breakthroughs each of us must:

- Want freedom from whatever holds us back from lives of fulfillment—whether it's our own fears and self-preservation, or outside forces such as dominating leaders, poor economic status, addiction, or some other factor.
- Have a longing for peace, growth, love, friendship, fulfillment.
- Be willing to risk what you have, fight through change, and work for something better.

What about you?

- What do you want freedom from?
- What are you longing for?
- Are you willing to take risks to gain it?

I work with many leaders who want to break through to a higher quality of leadership and life. They all have fears. Each experiences turmoil and even chaos as the result of letting go.

Our leadership company has developed some tools for helping them be successful. Let's look at them.

There is nothing better than having someone who is invested in your success and unafraid to give you honest feedback to help you break through your walls.

Tools for Breaking Through

- Line up a great friend, a life coach, or a leadership counselor—There is nothing better than having someone who is invested in our success and unafraid to give you honest feedback to help you break through your walls. If you don't have someone, find someone. At GiANT we use confidants to help leaders. I talk with one of our coaches, Dr. Jarrod Spencer, on a regular basis. He helps me work through my limitations and break through my own self-preservation (www. giantimpact.com can lead you to a coach, if needed).
- Weigh the pros and cons—Assessing the advantages and disadvantages of making a change will help you see which path offers the most rewards over the long term. Write down both the short-term and long-term consequences of either staying with the status quo or making a leap. Typically, this jolts people into wanting to change their path.
- Picture the life you want—After you write your list of consequences, take a few moments to describe the most fulfilling life imaginable. List the potential rewards that come from risking a change and then claim that life as a reality.

When you take a risk and break through to a better life, you will find the freedom exhilarating. Yet freedom doesn't come without sacrifice and even pain. Theodore Roosevelt, the twenty-sixth president of the United States, was a timid, nervous, and self-conscious boy who struggled with asthma. To gain strength, he exercised and took boxing lessons. He could have stayed in bed, but he was willing to work hard to break through to a better life. The encouragement and love of his father helped him to overcome his physical ailments and embrace a physically active life of adventure and risk.

It takes such dedication and desire to break through to a better life. You have to make the decision to commit and then take action. While the potential rewards may far outweigh the risks, the fact remains that thousands upon thousands of potentially great leaders never make the move because they are afraid of the unknown.

Hindrance to Action

So what keeps you from breaking through? There are several reasons why people resist.

- Unawareness—Some leaders don't fully understand the implications of their influence and the fact that they are supposed to impact others positively.
- Fear of change—Admit it: change is hard. Most leaders are so afraid of losing power, status, or income that they would rather stay in miserable jobs than make a leap to something better.
- Too far gone—A few leaders have serious baggage or bad

work records, and they don't want to give up security for an uncertain future. These leaders let their pasts dictate and limit their futures.

- Uncertainty—Many leaders want to be a positive influence but do not have the first inkling of how to do it. They don't know that they can be trained to serve others rather than themselves.

Inhibited or Prohibited

Most leaders who are self-centered and dissatisfied with their lives claim that they can't serve others because they are prohibited by outside factors such as family responsibilities or financial concerns. But more often than not, they are inhibited by their own fears and insecurities.

Prohibited is when someone else tells you that you can't do something.
Inhibited is when you tell yourself that you can't do something.

Your inhibitions can severely limit your capacity to lead. Have you ever watched a quarterback struggle to find a receiver even though there's a tight end wide open in the end zone? You yell at the TV in frustration, but you know it's a whole lot easier being an armchair quarterback than the real deal on the field.

In the same way, others may tell you that your fears and insecurities are holding you back, but you can't see it. We are often blind to our inhibitions because we've lived with them so long, or we're in denial. Many of my clients have all that it takes to be great and nurturing leaders, but they can't overcome long-held inhibitions.

Others can point out to you self-defeating behaviors and attitudes, but only you can take the actions necessary to break through to a more productive and fulfilling life. I was one of those leaders who felt inhibited but wasn't sure how to break through. The taxicab crash in Cancún nearly killed me, but in the end it made me stronger.

My near-death experience opened my eyes to the life I was living and to the life I wanted to live. I realized that I'd put my ladder against the wrong wall. Instead of striving for "success" and all of its trappings, I realized that what really would fulfill me was to be a positive influence on the lives of everyone around me. I gained perspective. I embraced my faith. I was reminded of the importance of being God's man, a good husband, and a good father. My accident gave me the opportunity to reset my priorities.

There is great benefit in breaking through. You should not presume it will be easy, but there is no limit to the joy, gratification, and impact you can have by getting to the other side—not only for you but for everyone you come in contact with as well.

While the focus here has been on your breakthrough, some of you may be wondering how you can help someone else discover and break through his or her own walls of self-preservation.

This is a delicate process, as we all have things that we protect. The best way to uncover the walls in someone else is to ask the person, "What are you afraid of losing?" Generally, the walls of self-preservation match the answers to this question. Writing them down and showing the leader generally leads to a breakthrough. However, to further drive home how self-preservation is affecting them, have him or her list how this overprotection is undermining his or her performance in his or her everyday life. Remember, you can't help others until you have helped yourself dismantle your own walls. The same process can then be used for you.

There is no better way to see a breakthrough than to spend time undercover in your own business.

Undercover Boss

Joel Manby, CEO of Herschend Family Entertainment (HFE), headquartered in Atlanta, did just that. Joel had the opportunity to go undercover inside his company, which operates twenty-six amusement parks across the country. His experience was both eye opening and encouraging.

Joel is a respected business leader who rose from a humble upbringing to the top of his industry. He moved up the management ranks at Saturn automobile manufacturers and went on to head a competitor, Saab North America. He was successful in his career but came to feel that the pressures of his job were hurting his relationship with his family. His wife agreed that Joel needed a breakthrough, and she supported him in finding his way to a better and more balanced life.

Joel stepped back and assessed where he was and where he wanted to go. He realized that he had to give up what he had achieved in order to claim what he really wanted. In walking away from his career in the automotive industry, Joel risked a great deal, but he gained even more. He refocused his energy on his relationship with his wife and family. Once he'd let go of his secure job—a very risky move—Joel freed himself for new opportunities, which led to his joining HFE, a company founded by two liberated leaders with a desire to have a positive impact on others.

Recently Joel and his company were profiled on the reality TV show *Undercover Boss*. In the episode, you could see Joel's humility and his desire to be a true positive influence to his employees. In one case, he met an employee whose house had been damaged by storms. You could see the pain and empathy in Joel's eyes as he listened to this man describe the challenges of repairing his home. Joel then explained to his employee that the company had a foundation designed to help team members dealing with financial challenges and personal crises.

As Joel worked undercover in his own company, he learned just how much its employees valued leaders who valued them and stepped up to assist them in time of need. Later Joel told me that he never could have come to the aid of employees in his old job, with his old attitude.

The television show highlighted the benefits of Joel's breakthrough, not just for him and his family but also for everyone in his circle of influence. Joel Manby is a true positive influence and a liberating leader.

With his success in mind, think about how you too can break through to a better life, and a more positive and influential level of leadership:

- What will your breakthrough be?
- Where will it occur if it hasn't already?
- How will you bring a breakthrough into your work world?

Culture Breakthrough

Our mission at GiANT is to "transform the leadership culture of America."

We realize that statement is bold, even a bit grandiose. But we provide practical action steps to back it up. By impacting leaders across America, our ultimate goal is to transform the culture of corporations and other organizations in this country.

Make no small plans, right? There are "only" about 30 million companies in the United States. We decided that to impact the leadership culture of America, we wanted to transform the culture of organizations within our own country. In order to do that we must create an opportunity to awaken, encourage, and resource the leaders themselves. If just one leader breaks through the walls of self-preservation, then we can change the level of influence in many other lives, starting with his or her employees. One person can change the trajectory of impact on another's life, and that person, in turn, can impact others in a similar manner. Carried forward, the implications are amazing!

One person can change the trajectory of impact on another's life and that person, in turn, can impact others in a similar manner. Carried forward, the implications are overwhelming!

We train leaders so that they can lead by example and inspire others.

- We do not need more political figures consumed with their own status, power, or financial well-being.
- We do not need more CEOs who put their own welfare above that of their company and their employees.

- We do not need more managers focused solely on their bonus checks and quotas, without consideration of the men and women who also aspire to better lives.
- We need breakthroughs!

To change the world, we need leaders who want to contribute to the greater good. We need leaders longing for more authenticity and less interested in preserving themselves; everyday leaders who want to build trustworthy relationships.

We need leaders longing for more authenticity and less interested in preserving themselves; everyday leaders who want to build trustworthy relationships.

The ground rules of leadership have changed. When the walls of self-preservation come down, true influence occurs. This begins a lifestyle of leadership. Real change comes when you get real. Yet influence begins when you give yourself to others. This is the heralding of significance and the dawn of a new style of leadership.

CHAPTER 7

INFLUENCE IS POWER

Leadership is the act of leading men and women to take unified action in accomplishing a common goal. Influence is what benevolent leaders wield to empower their teams to take action so that they can accomplish organizational or personal objectives. To influence someone, a leader leverages power. Again, this influence is amoral—it can be positive or negative influence for a positive or negative result.

Dwight D. Eisenhower provides a great example of someone who executed positive influence throughout his career. He was fifty-one years old before he made any significant military decisions. For almost thirty years, he studied and learned in the classroom and in the field. He was diligent, and he became competent and reliable. The famed General Douglas MacArthur called him "the best officer in the army."

General George Marshall sent Eisenhower to London to head the American military headquarters during World War II. He was chosen for his ability to connect with the British and because he was strong enough to handle forceful leaders such as the US

Army's General George S. Patton, British military commander Sir Bernard Montgomery, and General Charles de Gaulle of France. History shows that Eisenhower was the perfect man for the job.

At the core of Eisenhower's personality was a desire to do the right thing. He had experienced the abuse of power, often noting that he'd once played for a football coach who was more concerned about winning games than developing young men with character. Eisenhower was always aware that a leader could use power to destroy or to build. Despite many challenges and complexities, he led the Allied cause against the Axis powers and became one of the most decorated war heroes in US military history.

After serving as the thirty-fourth US president, from 1953 to 1961, Eisenhower took pride in his concern for his troops, boasting, "The United States never lost a soldier or a foot of ground in my administration. People ask how it happened—by God, it didn't just happen, I'll tell you that."

President Eisenhower used his influence and power for the betterment of the country. Leaders who leverage influence and harness power for the best interests of others are revered, successful, and significant.

Leaders who leverage influence and
harness power for the best interests of others are revered,
successful, and significant.

In our GiANT leadership survey, we asked more than one hundred significant business and community leaders to tell us what they believed to be the characteristics of an influencer:

- "Influencers see the whole, the greater good, not just their own tight circle of self-concerns."
- "Influencers are listeners. They value input, weigh both the words and the emotion behind them, and they build upon the thoughts and ideas of others without seeking credit. Because they are good listeners, they are often turned to for advice."
- "Influencers believe that 'People don't care how much you know until they know how much you care.' Influencers learn to care, and they are willing to convey that care."
- "Influencers have the ability to get others to join their causes—some by charisma and others by asking for help. In either case, influencers are moving in a direction for the specific cause to get better and better."
- "An influencer must recognize his ability to move people to action. Sometimes this may even involve a challenge— 'Courageous leaders ask for the courageous from those they lead.'"
- "Influencers are often the best storytellers. Sometimes they express it in a narrative, but often they connect people with a larger movement—giving life purpose, making sacrifice meaningful, and providing a renewable energy source."

The Flow of Influence

Influence is about power. Before you can become a leader, you need to determine how you will use your power.

Influence is a flow. Like a river, it has the ability to sustain life and grow people and places. Yet influence can also bring destruction down on others, leaving people damaged or even useless. A practical example is Zimbabwe, once the crown of Africa, which has now become a wasteland of impoverishment and unemployment as their president Robert Mugabe has desolated the land with his corruption and authoritarian nature.

It is important to understand that power must be controlled. Boundaries are imperative if you are to be a leader of character whose authority is respected.

I've already defined influence, but how does influence play out in the work world for the majority of Americans? Is influence applied in a draconian style of heavy rule, calm management from a kind boss, or is it merely part of a process for doing whatever it takes to get what you want?

I once heard a television reporter offer this assessment of a top-level White House staffer who was leaving one job to take another: "While he was a most boastful man who could bully and harass people to get what he wanted, he will be missed by the administration because of his productivity."

Apparently, leaders in that administration were allowed to bully and harass people as long as they were productive? Leadership is influence. Influence is power. In wielding that power, a leader can choose to use it in one of two ways:

To empower and liberate or
To overpower and dominate

Some people know exactly who they are and which style they embrace. Most can also accurately describe the leadership styles they admire or distrust.

Empowering leaders tend to be very self-aware. Their intent is to use their skills to serve and benefit others.

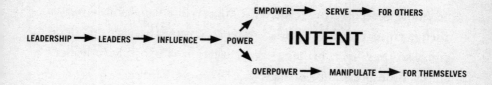

Overpowering leaders are focused on pursuing and accomplishing their own goals.

An executive in his late forties once told me that he hated who he had become. He had achieved his goals, but he'd done it by bullying and intimidating his team members. Although he'd accomplished his mission, no one respected or liked him—and, more importantly, he didn't like or respect himself.

He shared his feelings in a moment of vulnerability. Yet when I tried to influence him and guide him to a better path, he returned to his bullying ways. Eventually he was fired. In the end, his leadership was more disruptive than productive. This man was not prepared to handle the power entrusted to him as a top executive.

Overpower

To overpower is to subdue or control someone through manipulation or coercion. It is typically done for the benefit of the person in control. Overpowering normally leads to limiting productivity, as people either become enslaved or unable to fully deploy their skills. They will, many times, work in fear of the response from the overpowering leader. Overpowering leadership suppresses people and prevents them from performing with enthusiasm and creativity. Fear may motivate people for a time, but ultimately it is destructive and self-defeating.

Some overpowering leaders use this style unconsciously out of their own fear of failure. They want to ensure they get "it" done right, so they micromanage every situation. This style of leadership is widespread, unfortunately.

Then there are leaders who overpower their team members as a conscious strategy. They have no other way to accomplish their tasks and to motivate employees than to bully and overpower. They most likely worked under this style of leadership themselves, and they pass it along daily. Empowering others seems like a sign of weakness to these leaders as they may believe that giving someone else power may be paving the way for their own professional demise.

A Run-In with the Armenian Mafia

I've experienced the blunt trauma of overpowering leadership in some unique ways, especially during my years as an American entrepreneur living in crazy Mafia-plagued Russia. We lived in a modest flat in the middle of the capital city. An Armenian crime syndicate lived and ran their operations on the first floor. Andik was the boss. Needless to say, his Mob management style wasn't based on a model of empowerment. Andik was a Dominator, a bully, and a thug.

One brutal wintry night, we experienced his thuggery first-hand. I answered a knock on the door, and found Andik's wife, Emma, beaten severely and pleading for help.

"Andik is trying to kill me," she said in Russian. "He thinks I set him up to be killed. Protect me, please!"

Several scenarios raced through my mind—none of them with happy endings. Then Emma added one more valuable piece of information.

"They will come after me here."

"Great," I said under my breath.

Mark, my business partner, helped me find a place to hide the mobster's bloodied wife. Minutes later, Andik's goons rapped on the door with guns packed.

"We know she is here!"

I opened the door despite my fear. The goons made it clear that they believed Emma was inside, and that if I didn't hand her over, it wouldn't be good for us.

I refused to acknowledge that Emma was inside. So for the next three hours, the mobsters did their best, and worst, to terrorize us. Mark gave them a very slow tour of the place, while I kept moving Emma to different hiding places.

It was a cat and mouse game, and we were not in control.

Mark was doing a good job keeping the bad guys busy. I thought I'd found a good hiding place for her behind a washing machine in our large bathroom. While I was stashing Emma there, the goons demanded that I open the bathroom door. They'd checked every other room in the place by that point.

The only thing I could think to do was to pretend I'd been taking a shower. So, I stripped down to my boxers and doused myself with water. (The CIA will not be recruiting me anytime soon.)

I decided to counter their bullying with righteous indignation. I opened the bathroom door and demanded that they leave my home.

My bluff worked. The mobsters backed off. One of them even offered an apology. Someone later suggested that it was the sight of me in my boxers that frightened them. Whatever the reason, they went away and did not return. I retrieved Emma from the bathroom, helped her clean her wounds, and, later that night, engineered her safe exit from the building.

A few weeks later, gunshots tore through Andik's apartment. The next day, a new flock of goons moved in. That's pretty much what happens sooner or later to anyone who attempts to lead through intimidation.

Overpowering leadership brings diminishing returns. It is a selfish ploy and, ultimately, an ineffective approach in business, just as it is in relationships. Those being bullied will eventually flee or revolt when the opportunity arises.

Dominator

Dominating leaders use their influence to manipulate people to follow their own agenda. The typical goal of the Dominator is the pursuit of control, money, fame, and the status that comes with power. The end result of this style of leadership is generally very harmful. Dominators can ruin good people. Their actions often only heighten public cynicism toward leadership, which is difficult to counter and rarely goes away.

A dominating, overpowering leader uses influence to

- manipulate others;
- focus solely on his or her own success;
- control the lives of others;
- validate himself or herself;
- use people and their talents for his or her own benefit;
- create a demeaning culture that fosters divisiveness;
- enslave others mentally and emotionally.

Manipulation is the primary tool of the Dominator. Most overpowering leaders tend to master manipulation to accomplish their objectives. Manipulation involves using persuasion or pressure upon another person, normally through deception or exploitation. Manipulative tools include inauthentic praise, bribery, or fear-based coercion.

President Lyndon B. Johnson was known as an adept manipulator. He basked in the role and succeeded at manipulating people despite widespread awareness of his methods. By all accounts, President Johnson was a bully, too. He would dominate people by finding fault in them consistently. He would use his height to hover over people and display his power to them. Domination was his style of leadership and he wielded it on most occasions with most of the people he touched.

I would never want these words spoken of me, yet the late President Johnson was often described in these terms. Johnson was an old-school Dominator who proudly used manipulation to enforce his agenda and protect his power.

Too often, Johnson and others of his ilk are considered "typical" leaders—even role models—when, in fact, Dominators and manipulators are failed leaders because of their crude methods. They leverage power for all the wrong reasons and for their own selfish purposes. Those who are subjected to their manipulation rarely walk away feeling that they've benefited in any way.

Still, Dominators exist in every industry, in every city, and in every country today. They are often insecure yet oversecure; consuming yet consumed. From Bernie Madoff to corporate executives at Enron to the next example coming to a newspaper stand near you next month. These poor examples spawn cynicism and distrust of those with positions of authority and power in government and industry.

The world could use more liberating leaders, no doubt about that. I encourage you to seek out Liberators as role models and mentors. Spend as much time in their company as you can. And while you're at it, if you come across a Dominator, run!

On my blog, jeremiekubicek.com, I receive many inquiries asking how to handle Dominators. While I am not an expert on bullies, I do understand the oppression and hopelessness that comes when someone is employed in such a negative environment. I normally advise them to "run," simply because, in my opinion, life is too short to waste any amount of time in a toxic atmosphere. If they can't leave their job, I suggest they change the patterns of work even more intentionally to avoid the negativity that could affect their health and emotions.

A GOOD EXAMPLE OF A BAD EXAMPLE

Before a flight from Atlanta to a conference, I went to the Delta Sky Club to grab a snack. Unfortunately, I sat near a pair of salesmen who appeared to be Dominators of a high degree. One of the men was talking to a prospective client on the phone. Before and after the conversation, the salesmen discussed their plans to secure this prospect's business. I was appalled at their approach to business.

Before the call, one salesperson turned to the other and said, "Watch this. I'm gonna show you how to get business done." He dialed the number on his cell phone. As they talked, the salesman told his prospect, "Have I got an offer you can't refuse! You like NASCAR, don't you? Yeah, I thought so." He winked at his colleague. "I have box seats ready for you and one other person. Not only that, but we will pick you up and take care of the whole weekend."

Then he threw this kicker into the mix: "And, if you want to, we can take care of that 'one more,' if you know what I mean. We can arrange for a new girlfriend for you on our dime."

I couldn't believe what I was hearing. This was all happening within earshot of everyone around. The Liberator in me wanted to jump up, grab the phone, and say, "Don't do it! I know you don't know me, but all of us in the Sky Club know that these two jerks are setting you up so they can manipulate you."

As the salesman tried to close the deal, the prospect on the other end of the phone apparently chimed in that his wife wouldn't appreciate him getting a new girlfriend.

"Well, uh, you don't need to even think about that. Just bring your wife, and you two have fun on us. We will take care of all of the expenses," the salesman promised.

As they hung up, the salesman high-fived his colleague.

"I think we've got another one in the bag," he gloated. "This is too easy."

These two guys went on to discuss what type of women they preferred, as if they were billionaire playboys.

I was so disturbed by their display of unethical behavior that I considered whether to say anything, write them a note, or simply leave. I pulled out my journal to make notes just as they headed for their gate. There would be no confrontation that day except in my mind.

Their behavior was a model for coercive and abusive sales techniques. They were all about the transaction and short-term gains with apparently little thought about the potential long-term repercussions. How could this potential client ever trust salesmen who were so blatantly offering to manipulate him with gifts?

Sadly, this corrupt approach to business occurs all too often. True leadership and the exercise of influence are a very different deal. I am not here to judge these men. I *am* judging their style of leadership, though. Their actions were an abuse of influence that only further seared cynicism and skepticism into the minds of those who observed their actions and behavior. So let's address what to do when you encounter dominating leadership.

WHAT DO I DO IF MY BOSS IS A DOMINATING LEADER?

For many people in the workplace, dominating leaders are an everyday reality. My advice to you is to first check yourself. Understand what you can control and what you can't control. You can first control your attitude, your responses, and your communication. It may also be helpful to find a confidant to discuss the process with to ensure you are presenting yourself well.

Once you have walked through this process, then you can address your boss. Try to understand your boss's perspective. Where are the pressures coming from? Serve your boss for a period of time. Whatever you do, stay in control of your emotions during this process. If nothing changes and you are in a dire position, then look for a different position or transfer for the benefit of everyone, including yourself.

WHAT CAN I DO IF I REALIZE THAT I AM A DOMINATING LEADER?

You have already begun. Self-awareness is stage one. If you have been dominating in the way that you lead, admit it. Now complete the following sentence: "If I continue to lead and live like this, I will negatively affect____, and it will affect me by____."

List the consequences and then flip it by asking yourself the opposite: "If I change to become a liberating leader, it will bring the following rewards to me and the people around me."

Find a trusted confidant or executive coach to help walk you through the process of change.

OVERCOMING OVERPOWERING LEADERSHIP

My entrepreneurial ventures in Russia were made possible by the fact that the oppressive, overpowering leadership practiced there for seventy years or more was essentially overthrown. I found that the Russian people had been controlled and subdued to such an extent that, in the first six months of a new democracy, they didn't know how to respond. They were overwhelmed by their freedom. For the first time in their adult lives, they were free to think for themselves rather than being coerced to perform a certain way.

One day I stood outside our flat in the center of Moscow watching Russian men work up the courage to rip out the Big Brother–ish "music" boxes installed in every apartment, which allowed the KGB to listen inside apartments and maintain control. Our flat had one until we accidentally removed it. Our small revolt was symbolic of a much larger revolution against overpowering leadership.

Dictatorial rule is the tool of lazy leaders. It is easier for them to overpower than to empower.

Empower

To empower is to enable someone else to accomplish something. It is a transfer of authority. The very word itself is positive. Empowering others typically yields greater returns and goodwill.

Think about how this applies to your approach to leadership. Each of us has been empowered by someone, at some point—perhaps a teacher, a parent, or a boss who has encouraged you or provided you with opportunities.

My father empowered me to drive a tractor for the first time on our family's farm in central Oklahoma when I was thirteen years old. While I was excited, I was also very tense. With empowerment comes responsibility. Yet empowerment fully realized leads to growth. While my father was empowering me to help the family farming operation, he was also teaching me skills and helping me discover who I was as a young man.

Giving orders and directions is not empowerment.
Rather, an empowering leader trains, mentors, and apprentices
someone to help him or her grow.

Giving orders and directions is not empowerment. Rather, an empowering leader trains, mentors, and apprentices someone to help him or her grow. To empower is a positive act of service for the benefit of others, and it should be the goal of every leader.

To empower is an art and a science. Managing power is very difficult. Authority is accompanied by responsibility, which can be difficult for some to share and for others to accept. Have you ever heard someone say, "The only way to get things done is to do it myself?" That's not an empowering leader talking. With empowerment comes trust in other people. Some personality types have more difficulty sharing power because they trust only themselves to get the job done.

I think of empowerment as investment and diversification. To empower others means that you are helping people improve their capacity to share their gifts as they perform tasks needed by the organization. This is diversifying team strengths as people are given the opportunity to grow.

Empowering leaders are rare these days but highly appreciated. A few years ago, my company had the privilege of hosting an interview with former British prime minister Tony Blair in his stately London office, which was once home to the US ambassador to England and the second president of the United States, John Adams, and his wife, Abigail. Dr. Henry Cloud interviewed the former prime minister. As I listened in, I was struck by Mr. Blair's practical wisdom and his desire to empower others. It seemed that his many years in politics had made him better in his philosophy of what he believed, rather than being worn out from a political life of serving everyone's interests. Here is his take on empowerment from his memoir, *A Journey: My Political Life:* "The only way we [Progressives] win is by being the party of empowerment, and that requires a state that is more minimalist and strategic; that is about enabling people, about developing their potential but not constraining their ambition, their innovation, their creativity."

The Liberator

As you might expect, liberating leaders are quite opposite from Dominators. Liberators use their influence to serve their team members while unleashing their talents. They are facilitators who seek to accomplish organizational objectives and the personal goals and self-fulfillment of individuals on their team. Liberators leave a legacy of accomplishment, respect, and gratitude.

A liberating, empowering leader uses influence to

- be responsive to those she leads;
- focus on others' successes;
- fight for others when necessary;
- encourage the release of other people's gifts;
- nurture liberating leaders of the future.

Supporting and strengthening others are primary goals of a Liberator. To liberate is to empower others to fulfill and exceed their potential, and to use their strengths for the benefit of the team. The process nurtures self-confidence and individual growth by allowing others to make mistakes and to learn from them without being threatened or condemned.

I have witnessed that Liberators are not afraid of protecting or freeing those they support. Liberators tend to have their priorities straight. With them, wisdom is a currency that they disburse daily.

A REAL-LIFE LIBERATOR

I worked for an amazing family company when I was in my mid-twenties. Jacks Merchandising and Distribution was led by Kent Humphreys, a Liberator to the core. During the years that I worked for him, I found Kent to be a brilliant thinker and a man of utmost character. The company was special not because of what it did but because of a culture that encouraged employees to be the "best version of themselves," as my friend, author Matthew Kelly, likes to say.

Kent isn't afraid to fight for the benefit of others when necessary, and he always helps others out of a spirit of love. For me,

Kent was a great example of an empowering leader who wanted the best for his people and the organization. Several years later, he sold the business to a national firm that intended to roll up around twenty distributors, package them, and then sell them to a larger organization. After the sale, I went to work for the new entity. My goal was to serve the new owners in the same manner that I had tried to serve Kent, even though once the Liberator left, the culture changed to a traditional style of control and overpowering leadership.

The benefits I received from Kent personally were innumerable. He showed me how to liberate as we served clients, helped employees, and even encouraged vendors. Not only did he counsel me, Kent continued to encourage me and invest in me long after we stopped working together. He's like that for most everyone. He is still there for me whenever I need his advice.

The good news is that Liberators like Kent are more prevalent than you might think. They are just quieter than Dominators by nature, so they don't always receive the attention they deserve. When Liberators lead, things tend to run smoothly. Thus, you rarely hear of them. Dominators, on the other hand, tend to be so destructive and disruptive that they are hard to ignore.

Empowering, liberating leaders tend to be very concerned about the lives of their team members. Some corporate Liberators I've known include Dan Cathy of Chick-fil-A, Mike Duke of Wal-Mart, and David Green of Hobby Lobby.

I remember interviewing David years ago and coming away amazed at what he and his family have built at Hobby Lobby. This $2 billion arts and crafts company started in 1972 with one store in Oklahoma City. Today it has over 460 stores in thirty-eight states. While Hobby Lobby's continued growth is significant, its desire for influence is equally inspiring. The Green family has expanded its reach into helping the next generation through giving money, time, and new ideas to a few private universities as they innovate the collegiate experience. The company culture is focused on growth and influence and empowering its leaders to lead by example and to serve those they lead.

THE POWER OF EMPOWERMENT

The biblical account of Moses encountering his father-in-law, Jethro, in the desert offers a great example of empowerment leadership. Moses was leading thousands of Israelites out of Egypt through the desert when Jethro, his father-in-law and former boss for forty years, came to visit him. Each asked the other how things were going—the good and the bad. This is the sign of a trusting relationship.

The next day, Jethro observed his son-in-law acting as a judge, ruling on disputes of the everyday leaders. It took him all day to finish hearing all the disagreements. Jethro was dumbfounded by the commitment.

"What are you really accomplishing here?" he asked Moses. "Why are you doing this yourself while everyone stands around you from morning until evening?"

Moses tried to rationalize his actions by saying that he was responsible for the people and that arbitrating disputes was his duty.

Jethro rebutted, "This is not good! You are going to wear yourself out—and the people, too. This job is too much for you to handle all by yourself. Select some capable, honest leaders from among you. Appoint them as leaders over groups of one thousand, one hundred, fifty, and ten. They should be available to solve the problems instead of you." From this moment, middle management was born.

Jethro advised Moses to let others help him carry the load of leadership, which would ease everyone's burden. "If you follow my advice, you will be able to endure the pressures, and all these people will be in peace," he told Moses.

The wise leader understands that sharing the burden benefits the entire team over the long term. Empowering others makes tasks manageable while also allowing team members to sharpen their skills and build upon their strengths. When a leader refuses to share the load, he brings disservice to the organization because those on his team are not allowed to develop their own leadership skills, and the next generation of leaders are not developed properly for future organizational success.

Moses listened to his father-in-law. He chose capable men and appointed them as leaders just as Jethro recommended. They brought the most pressing cases to Moses, but took care of all the smaller matters. Soon after this, Moses said good-bye to Jethro. I am sure that the hug was long and the appreciation high.

To empower is a gift of leadership. Accomplishing goals while earning the gratitude of an engaged team creates a lasting legacy of great leadership. The leader who hogs the work and the glory may reap short-term benefits, but over the long term he creates a cynical workforce that is reluctant to follow and ill prepared to lead.

Respect is a dividend earned when you manage power and authority with grace and caring so that your team grows its capacities while serving the needs of the organization.

The Colors of Domination and Liberation

World War II was essentially a battle between the forces of liberation and the forces of domination. This devastating conflict was

triggered by the aggressive actions of Nazi leader Adolf Hitler, an insecure, manipulative dictator and Dominator. I believe that 99 percent of the human population would agree with that assessment. This man is one of the clearest examples of a dominating leader in our modern history.

Hitler and his Nazi followers spread terror around the world in rampages and slaughters that resulted in the deaths of more than sixty million people from fifty-seven countries. The Third Reich lost approximately eight million people. Its legacy, and that of its Axis allies, would be to annihilate close to 4 percent of the entire world population by 1945. Ultimately, those casualties would include Hitler as well.

As one Dominator was defeated, another was emerging. Joseph Stalin and his Red Army of Soviet Communists swept into Europe from the East, claiming that they were merely protecting themselves from future wars. His legacy, which already included millions of deaths, was the Cold War dividing line, the Iron Curtain, which left Western Europe liberated, free, and thriving, and Eastern Europe dominated, controlled, and depleted.

The map opposite shows the dominating aftereffects of World War II, with light gray representing liberation in Western Europe and dark gray representing the domination in Eastern Europe. Liberation empowers people through freedom to thrive, whereas domination overpowers people with control.

While living in Russia just one year after the Soviet empire imploded, I observed and dealt with this firsthand. I watched the aftermath and repercussions of a seventy-year system of control and domination that did nothing to advance the people physically, mentally, socially, or spiritually. Manipulation and suppression of individual freedoms had paralyzed the economy and the national spirit.

Each week, I'd have lunch with a client's employee named Sasha—a former worker within the KGB, the Soviet government's secretive security and police agency that conducted international and domestic spying operations. Sasha was inviting and confident. He had an infectious spirit and a keen mind that loved freedom. He told me that while working for the KGB, he was continually coerced by his supervisors; and he, in turn, used coercion on those under his control during his years with the agency.

The aftereffects of this oppressive system were evident in all aspects of society. By the early 1990s, Russians were like prisoners coming out of decades of confinement and into the light. Freedom was so foreign to them that they didn't really know what to do with it. Our apartment looked out upon the looming Stalin Tower, one of the tallest buildings in Russia. Often, I would open my window and stare at the ominous structure. My job was to train young Russian leaders in ethical business practices. Yet here were the remnants of decades of Communist oppression. You could see the oppression in the eyes of the everyday citizen. Yuri was one of the few exceptions.

Gray versus green. Empowering versus overpowering leadership. Dominators are like strip miners, who scrape the landscape clean of life and leave it gray and lifeless. Liberators nurture the soil, green the landscape, and create self-sustaining life.

Is There a Middle Ground?

What if you see yourself as neither a Liberator nor a Dominator but as someone whose leadership style lies between those polar opposites? I have found there are truly very few examples of the extremes of Liberators and Dominators. The vast majority of leaders today have a style that falls somewhere near the middle.

How many people do you know who truly dominate an organization or a community? I have no doubt that there are office tyrants and city council dictators to be found. However, it's rare to find one of them erecting an Iron Curtain at city hall or corporate headquarters. Then again, how many true Liberators do you know? How many people do you know who understand true influence? How many empower other leaders consistently, day in and day out?

The fact is that our leadership culture is filled with scores of leaders who neither fully empower nor fully overpower but do both—even in the very same day. Or hour. In fact, I would venture to say that most leaders occupy this space.

Many leaders practice both styles, switching back and forth, wielding power day to day in whatever manner suits them and their purposes. It would be naïve to think that abuses won't occur, but even the worst bully can change his ways. I've even known some leaders who empower at work and overpower at home. Conversely, there are some great leaders at home who are bullies in the office.

As a parent, a spouse, a boss, and a member of your community, you have the power to influence others for a lifetime. That's a powerful gift, and one you should use wisely and with great care.

Knowing Your Leader Type

We all have our moments when we act as Liberators or Dominators. Every leader can have good days and bad days. Yet most people have a tendency to lean in one direction or the other.

It is vital for you to begin understanding your leader type. However, most leadership training pays scant attention to developing the inner core—the heart and soul of being a leader. In traditional leadership training, such self-knowledge and character development are considered to be "soft skills," too "light and fluffy" for consideration. Most MBA schools offer very little time for such reflection and soul-searching. The emphasis is generally on hard skills: the traditional methods of manipulation that involve leading rather than influencing.

Our society as a whole has bought into the separation of private morality and public morality. Yet who you are impacts what you do.

What you believe affects how you act. The corruption of leadership in modern society—from the plethora of Ponzi schemes to rampant greed that brings down entire industries—offers ample evidence.

Leaders who are broken morally and spiritually are dangerous to their teams, to their communities, and to themselves. Broken moral codes lead to shattered professional codes.

Therefore, it is vital that you approach your leadership position fully aware of your own well-defined moral codes. Even if you don't feel strong in that area of your life, knowing your weak spots, your Achilles heel, is a strength. We all have weaknesses, and acknowledging them allows us to reduce risk and build on strengths.

THE TRAITS OF A LIBERATING LEADER

Every quest leads with a question, or two:

- Who is the best leader you have ever worked for or spent considerable time with?
- What leadership traits did that person exhibit?
- How did this admirable leader impact his or her team?

Now, let's look at the other side:

- Who was the worst leader you have every worked for or observed?
- What were this person's leadership traits?
- How did this poor leader impact the team and the business or organization?

It is important to understand that we are not judging these people but trying to learn from them. The intent is to clarify your own vision for the style of leadership you aspire to wield. As you may have determined, I advocate that you set your sights on becoming a liberating leader and a true influence. The keys to achieving this form of leadership include learning the following:

- Humble yourself.
- Empower others.
- Listen to emotions as well as words.
- Practice empathy.
- Lead others to success through a service mentality.

A LIBERATOR MUST FIRST BE LIBERATED

There is a starting place to true influence. To be significant in someone else's life means that something of significance has happened in your own life.

Every great leader is great because of his or her positive impact on others. Yet every great leader that I know of has undergone some dramatic change in perspective that altered his or her view of the world and enabled that person to serve others in profound ways.

I shared my own liberation story with you in chapter 2. Being crushed in a taxi while in a hurricane can affect your perspective of life and your priorities in a hurry. What is your liberation story? Quite humbly, I hope that this book may spark you to look at your story and make any necessary changes.

Most liberated leaders have similar stories:

- They were in control of their world.
- Their view of the world revolved around themselves.

- They treated others in their lives as supporting characters to their lead role.
- A negative event took place.
- They saw the reality of their lives and the potential for negative outcomes.
- Their weaknesses became more obvious.
- They gained a new perspective on life and what was most important to them.
- Their agendas changed as their intent became focused on those things that meant the most to them.
- They focused less on themselves and more on others.
- They experienced self-fulfillment in ways never imagined.

Understanding Power

Understanding power and where it comes from is crucial when discussing leadership. Each of us yields influence, whether positive or negative, with those we lead. That is why it is imperative to understand leadership styles, especially for those who aspire to lead the current and next generations.

Self-preserving leaders focus on protecting their status and security. This is the shifting middle ground of leadership; the space for the fearful and shortsighted. It may appear at first glance that their impact on others is neutral, but when you look deeper, you see that it is actually negative. They cause more harm than good.

This is precisely why I love history. There is no greater perspective on influence and life change than what history provides of leaders who tried, struggled, and were liberated—both in failure and in success. In failure there is great perspective. In triumph there is great perspective. Since life is a story, it is great to read others' stories so that we can hone our skills to benefit others.

There is no greater perspective on influence and life change than what history provides of leaders who tried, struggled, and were liberated—both in failure and in success.

Examples of leaders both good and bad are easily available online and in your favorite bookstore and local library. Studying these leaders can lead to self-knowledge. To understand true influence is to understand real motivation. Now is the time to begin leading for the better.

CHAPTER 8

IT'S ALL ABOUT RELATIONSHIPS

True influence is the everyday commerce of leadership. Once you get out of the transactional loop, you are free to enjoy the relationships of life that come with influence. Relationships then becomes the norm, not the exception.

Is there such a thing as a perfect relationship? "No," you may argue, "nothing can be perfect." While I agree with you, I will tell you that I believe it is possible to form strong bonds even in a world of greed, power, and corruption. These powerful relationships exist in business and in communities. How does this occur?

Once you free yourself by letting go of your own wants and needs and focusing on serving others, your vantage point changes. You will be free to serve and give without fear of losing. You will see other people's needs as joyful opportunities for service. It is possible to have empowering relationships in all aspects of life.

The influence model is a tool that can be used to help leaders move from mediocrity to a life of lasting impact. The model is built, established, and run on trust.

Influence requires commitment. This is precisely why most people do not have much impact: it costs something. In fact, every influential person in my life has sacrificed either time, energy, or effort to influence me.

Leaders do not fully control their influence. Yet living a life of impact means that influence is possible all of the time.

Learning Influence

Many men I've worked with have broken free of self-preservation and reached out—only to realize that they are fearful of the power their influence might have on others. It's such a foreign concept to them after years of focusing only on their own wants and needs. True influence means that you are willing to risk reaching out and giving of yourself, whether it's your time, your energy, or your money.

I once belonged to a group of middle-aged and senior CEOs who were tutored by a master influencer, entrepreneur Regi Campbell. His classes were designed to help us become better mentors at work, at home, and in life. Regi walked the walk. He gave freely of himself and his possessions. Each month he provided us with books, resources, and food during our sessions, all paid for out of his own pocket. Twice during our year of training, Regi hosted retreats, including one all-expenses-paid feast at his beach house on Pawleys Island, South Carolina.

Regi has been hosting groups like this several times a year for over a decade. What would possess him to give of himself so freely? I believe it is because he has learned what you and I need to learn:

Where you invest your influence, you invest your life.

Where you invest your influence, you invest your life.

My hope is that the influence model will help you think through the process of impacting others and help you change whatever you need to change about yourself so that you can be as free as Regi Campbell. Then return the favor to others to spread the influence.

We all need to earn a living so we can support ourselves and our dependents. Our businesses need money to survive. Yet think past the transaction for a moment. What would happen if you went above and beyond making money to impact the lives of your employees, customers, and vendors?

I have rarely met a successful entrepreneur who leaves money on the table. The vast majority of successful entrepreneurs I meet do routinely leave influence on the table, though, and lots of it. The current standard of leadership is focused on making money— a transactional frame of reference. Most of our education, training, and leadership principles are based on becoming better transaction experts, not influencers. This is not good enough for you. You need more. You want more.

The current method for training influence is to "fake it until you make it." I was first taught this in a sales school in my early twenties. The concept is to try to establish commonality. The attitude here is that half the world doesn't have good character and the other half doesn't know what it is doing. If you, as a leader, they say, can put both of these together, then you have positioned yourself for great success. We were trained to show that we were trustworthy and smart by giving people what they needed so that they would give us money or a commitment. Then we'd rush back to ring the bell and celebrate the transaction.

The problem with this philosophy is that it corrupts our youngest leaders into believing that sealing the deal is all that matters and that they should do whatever it takes to make it happen. One of the most successful reality shows, *The Apprentice*, teaches young leaders to do just that—do whatever you need to do to get a transaction, no matter the consequences. In the end, the best manipulator wins the prize. The show highlights lavish lifestyles and high-end perks as a lure to a style of influence that is self-serving and dominating.

A friend of mine encountered this in the real world when he visited a small used car lot to check out a sporty vehicle. The salesman who approached him struck up a conversation in which he mentioned that he'd once worked at a big dealership down the road. My friend noted that this particular dealership had a reputation for adding overpriced extra features like pinstriping and "upholstery sealant" to its new cars, while overcharging for mechanical repairs.

"Well, you may call that 'gouging,' but I call it 'doing business,'" the salesman said.

Needless to say, my friend looked elsewhere for his car.

This must stop. There is a different way . . . a new style of leader who is more benevolent and positive in influence. It is found on the other side of self-preservation. This leader's focus is on building mutually beneficial relationships by giving freely of God-given gifts. The real opportunity comes within the relationships that offer more than you would ever reap from an ordinary transaction.

It is a learned skill to give without seeking anything in return. Yet the rewards for giving so freely are valid and real. The biggest reward of all is true influence. What honor and significance there is when you know that you are impacting someone and bringing out his or her best!

Action No. 5: Pursue Relationship Before Opportunity

True influence is about establishing authentic relationships that far exceed any financial or personal opportunity. To do so is not easy because our self-preserving instincts often seem to get in the way. Consider how you approach business meetings. Do you think:

- What can I gain from these people?
- What is it that I want from them?
- How can I help them grow?
- What are they trying to accomplish?

I have found the first to be a primary question for most in business. It was certainly mine for most of my career. Mind you, I have always strived to be a person of character. However, my ambition and drive were so strong that while I was concerned about what others wanted, their needs were usually not my top priority.

There is a better way. To pursue a relationship for the other person's benefit, without focusing on your own needs, is an amazing way to work and live. Realize that I am a big fan of opportunity, but I believe opportunities come more readily to those who put others first.

Opportunities come more readily to those who put others first.

Relationships are the keys to opportunities because opportunity is a natural extension of goodwill. It is a paradox: when you pour yourself into serving others for their benefit, you gain good-will that yields the fruits of opportunity.

Building relationships before seeking rewards has become a mantra of our company, and GiANT sales teams have been trained to think this way. In 2007 we bought a very transactional-minded company. It was a good company, but the premise seemed to be selling tickets to events and selling books to those in attendance. I have nothing against that being a part of the business plan. However, I simply wanted to first seek true influence by building relationships rather than focusing on transactions.

Why? In business, transactions are fleeting, whereas relationships can last a lifetime. When you focus on relationships rather than deals, you have an opportunity to accomplish more over a longer period. In a transaction, you take away whatever someone pays, and that's the extent of your interaction. Relationships are gifts that keep on giving.

"Relationship before opportunity" is about giving before receiving, planting before harvesting, and serving before asking. The most important aspect of relationship building is to see that the other person's needs are met first. This has become the primary strategy of our business:

1. Relationship before opportunity.
2. In the opportunity, serve the relationship

American business leaders generally aren't naturals when it comes to focusing on relationships first. They are trained to seek short-term rewards instead of long-term relationships. Our relationships, therefore, become short and shallow. To truly be effective as a leader of lasting impact in our culture, it is imperative that you build deep, rich relationships in your professional and personal lives. Leadership comes alive when your relationships are more important than transactions.

I LIKE THE CONCEPT "RELATIONSHIP BEFORE OPPORTUNITY," BUT WHAT IF I AM NOT VERY GOOD AT IT AND ALSO HAVE EXTREME PRESSURE TO MAKE THINGS HAPPEN? WHAT DO I DO THEN?

First you need to understand that I am not asking you to become best friends with everyone you meet. On the contrary, I am asking you to work to become invested in those you lead. To be invested in someone and to put her best interests before your own creates the possibility of a mutually beneficial relationship. Here is one of my favorite quotes from Truett Cathy, the founder of the fast-food chain Chick-fil-A: "If you help people get what they want, they will help you get what you want." Focus on serving others first, and strong relationships will follow.

Tasks Versus Relationships

My business is built upon the heartening fact that so many leaders truly desire to improve their leadership and influence. So what holds them back? What is holding *you* back? Are you afraid of being seen as "soft"? Do you think that building relationships is a waste of time, when so much needs to be accomplished?

I find that some of our clients confuse the essential act of building relationships with the less essential practice of socializing at work. Relationships within your job can allow you to complete your work goals while also serving as a positive influence. This isn't about adding to your social calendar. It's about building mutual trust with your team members.

Too often, the day-to-day pressures of leadership can lead some to fall into the default mode of command-and-control-style leadership. It makes sense, when you think about it. People simply don't have the time to empower others when the pressure to perform is intense. Often they fear losing power if they don't wield it decisively.

In those situations, tasks often become more important than relationships. This is especially true for those who tend to be introverted. Extroverts are more naturally inclined to nurture relationships. The fact remains that to exercise true and lasting influence, you must empower rather than overpower your team.

Sharpening the axe may take time away from chopping, but the sharper blade allows you to make up for it once you return to the task, right? Many busy executives have difficulty taking the time to sharpen their leadership styles. The natural inclination is to keep your nose to the grindstone instead of the axe.

Yet there is no doubt that if a leader takes the time to empower others, he will make his job all the easier over the long term. Empowered teams increase their organization's efficiency and work capacity because the capacity and capabilities of those within the organization are themselves increased. Teams with strong and trusting relationships generally produce at higher levels, and their members don't experience the same rates of burnout that less cohesive teams experience.

You may ask, "How do I handle the pressure of authority when I have to hit numbers or quotas and manage people?"

Everyone must learn how to lead, but first you must choose what type of person, leader, and coworker you want to be. Do you remember the first time that you were handed authority over another person? What did it feel like? How did your attitude change?

The balance between managing tasks and managing people is difficult, especially if you tend to lean one way over the other.

Choose to liberate and empower your people, and I believe that you will begin to see positive results both in terms of progress on tasks and people management.

Empowerment takes time, but it works. Listening to your employees or staff is more time consuming than dictating to them, especially when the pressure is on. It is not natural to serve when you are striving to achieve. Some leaders find it easier to do things themselves rather than train others to accomplish the job. Great leaders, though, learn how to achieve while listening, relating, and serving. They understand influence and the importance of empowering others. They relinquish certain responsibilities to empower others to achieve more than they could have done for themselves.

The best leaders regularly self-assess by asking themselves hard questions and answering them honestly. Then the great leaders take thoughtful action. They continuously strive for perfection even while acknowledging that it may be unattainable.

By asking yourself whether you are empowering or overpowering, you open the door to honest self-examination and self-correction. You can choose to be one or the other, yet each style has ramifications. Choose the fruitful life of an influencer and invest in relationships.

The Deeper Relationship

In some cultures, relationships are more like gold than they are in the United States. The concept is unusual for Americans but worth considering. To form a deep relationship is to pledge a bond. Symbols of this include kids becoming "blood brothers," business partnerships, and even the ultimate partnership: marriage.

To develop a bond is serious business. The US Army pledges to "leave no man behind." That is a covenant requiring great commitment. My favorite movie, *We Were Soldiers*, highlights the special bond between Lieutenant Colonel Hal Moore and his men early in the Vietnam War. Before they head off to battle the Vietcong in the la Drang Valley, Moore, played by Mel Gibson, delivers the following inspirational speech:

> We're moving into the valley of the shadow of death, where you will watch the back of the man next to you, as he will watch yours. Let us understand the situation: we're going into battle against a tough and determined enemy. I can't promise you that I will bring you all home alive, but this I swear: when we go into battle, I will be the first one to set foot on the field, and I will be the last to step off. And I will leave no one behind. Dead or alive, we will all come home together. So help me, God.

Moore leads his men to victory after they are ambushed and seem to be in a hopeless situation. Each man follows the leader. This movie is so endearing to me because it explores the feelings of a man committed to his men. Throughout the film, Moore remains true to his covenant with his soldiers amid the chaos and horror of a battlefield.

Why is it so hard to commit to others in business or relationships? What are we really afraid of? Again, I think it's a matter of self-preservation for many people. Some fear that they don't have the resources, the tools, or the time to maintain a committed relationship. You might try asking yourself these questions before you make a decision to commit:

1. Influence Up—Am I willing to commit to the relationships with my board or mentors in my life?
2. Influence Across—Do my partners see my commitment levels to them? Am I "all in"?
3. Influence Down—Does my assistant know that I would do anything for her and her family? Would my employees and team members?

Forget Contracts

When a bond is in place in partnerships, with employees and within marriage, contracts are irrelevant. Those who put relationships before opportunities are trusting. Relationship-first means that you are more committed to the other person than any contract could bind you. You are willing to serve him or her above and beyond all else.

When you seek opportunity first, then contracts become the ultimate goal for sealing the deal. Every negotiation point and every conversation is intended to result in a signed contract. This is how most of the transactional world operates today.

What would it be like if you didn't have a contract, because relationships are more important? In my business dealings, we've found that deep relationships lead to such strong bonds that contracts become less important. While our business team signs agreements and contracts to set agreed-upon terms, we focus so much on the relationship that the contract process is no longer as significant.

The ultimate example of the poor intent of contracts comes from prenuptial marriage agreements. What signal does this send? What is the foundation of these relationships? Trust?

Prenup agreements are a reflection of self-centered individuals who enter into relationships only if they feel protected. It's not about giving of themselves. It's about guarding their interests first. This type of contract is not based on a covenant of trust. It's more of a self-preservation tool that indicates a deep and abiding lack of trust.

The Reason We Don't Commit

Apparently, committing to anything other than self-preservation is a challenge in our self-centered culture. Yet my own business has thrived since we've committed to "relationships first" as our philosophy. I find that ironic because many in business believe that the only way to attract opportunities is through aggressive transactional methods.

As a dedicated entrepreneur, I love opportunities. Most entrepreneurs are adept at finding opportunities where others see only problems or nothing at all. Our typical opportunities may be a new business, a potential new hire, or a strategic connection. Those with a transactional approach to business are often so hungry for opportunities that they pounce on them like predators. These overeager opportunity seekers stalk them with glazed eyes. Unfortunately, they often lose out on opportunities because they are self-preservationists who stress their own interests above all else.

I experienced this when dealing with an overly aggressive entrepreneur named Rick. He was constantly checking his traps for opportunities, and he made no apologies for it. His behavior was so over the top that others in our circles joked about his predatory ways. He was trapped in a vicious circle: the more he struggled in business, the more aggressively he pushed everyone he knew to create opportunities for him. Yet the harder he pushed, the more people resented his pushy communication style.

I tried to help him, advising him to ease up and build relationships before seeking opportunities, but he didn't get it.

"I'm not in it for the relationships. I already have all of those I need," he said. "I don't have time to commit to anything else."

Case closed.

Opportunities are more accessible when trusting relationships exist. Rick's disregard for relationships and his aggressive efforts to drum up business no doubt cost him opportunities.

Why Relationships First Is a Valid Approach

When you seek to build a relationship before mining for opportunities, you establish yourself as more genuine and trustworthy. Conversely, when someone senses that you are forever looking to cut a favorable deal rather than establish a lasting business or personal relationship, she may put up her own defenses.

One of our GiANT sales leaders, Jason, had to break away from the transactional approach to business when he first joined our team. He'd developed strong self-preservation instincts earlier in his career, and they were holding back a guy of great character and competence. He took my challenge to break through. Jason found that he still hits his sales number each month, but by investing in relationships first, he is experiencing long-term success as well as short term. It took a while for him to make the full transition, but he is reaping the rewards.

In fact, Jason has built such strong relationships that he is now a trusted confidant to many corporate leaders, who consult with him on how they can teach their team members what Jason learned. He often provides his clients with far more than the typical salesman offers, but he's found that the more he gives away, the more he sells!

There are many benefits to putting relationships first. Perhaps the greatest is the true and lasting friendships that you build along with your business relationships. For example, at GiANT, we have an annual client appreciation day. It is supposed to honor those we serve, but many of Jason's clients honored him instead. One client after another came up to me with comments such as, "I need to tell you about Jason. He is amazing!" This is the type of business approach everyone should have!

Jason serves his clients, and the bonds he forms with them create far more opportunities than he could ever manufacture by aggressively seeking transactions. When you build relationships first, the rewards extend beyond business and exceed all expectations.

Even when the opportunity does become available (which it invariably does), it is important to maintain the focus on the relationship. I consistently remind our team to serve the relationship first and foremost. It is the relationship that is most valuable—both to the organization and to the individuals they serve. When you seek the best for others and opportunities come, then it is imperative to continue to serve their best interests.

Jordan Zimmerman is the founder of Zimmerman advertising, which competes head to head with major New York advertising firms from its base in sunny Fort Lauderdale, Florida. His firm, the largest in South Florida and one of the largest in the nation, has landed huge clients such as Nissan USA, AutoNation, Dell, Party City, CARFAX, and Papa John's by relentlessly serving clients' needs first.

One of Zimmerman's methods for doing this is to send his own employees to work for the companies of prospective clients so that they learn the business from the inside out. The goal is to understand each client's business as well or better than the client himself, and then to serve those needs. This is not a benevolent policy; it's proven to be a very smart and profitable approach because of the mutual trust that is established and the long-term relationships that are built.

If you are leading an organization or responsible for serving clients in any way, here are some practical examples of how to pursue relationship before opportunity:

- Know their names and personal details so that you can keep the conversation genuine.
- Seek to know the personal side before the business side.
- Customers want pain to go away. Learn about their needs so that you can serve them.
- Help them with their issues. Add value by solving problems and maintaining relevance.
- Be available. Being there whenever your client needs you is an invaluable service.

Relationships are a competitive advantage, but only if you are honest about your motives and pure in your intent. In no way am I legitimizing forming relationships for the goal of growing a business. I am simply making the case here that deep relationships frequently lead to great opportunities that benefit everyone.

The change to a relational approach from a transactional approach can be difficult, but most people find that once they adjust, every aspect of their lives benefits. When change in a leader occurs, change in his or her world begins. Some leaders need to be awakened, while others simply need encouragement or tools to make the change effectively.

Each action we've discussed is an opportunity to expand your influence and improve your leadership. None, however, is more difficult—or more advantageous—than the next one.

Action No. 6: Give Yourself Away

The next level of influence is the most fun of all. It's based on the premise that it truly is better to give than to receive. In a self-preservationist's mind-set you can't give something without losing something. This is known as a "scarcity mentality."

This next stage of influence is based instead on an "abundance mentality," in which you believe that there are no limits on what you can give because there are no limits on what you can receive. So giving is not about losing something, it's about putting yourself and your gifts out there in the universe for the benefit of all.

Don't believe me that giving is better than getting? Try it.

Self-preservation is about getting and keeping. Fulfillment, however, lies in letting go and giving. Once you start, you won't be able to stop. Giving of yourself becomes a way of life.

Let me explain that when I say "giving," I mean it in the context of your work environment, not solely within your personal, civic, church, or charity life. I am talking about the giving that happens from nine to five every day.

If you are going to live a life of true influence, you will need to learn how to give of yourself and your talents. The problem is that, at times, you will want to hold on to the most important thing in your world: you.

To have true influence, you must embrace a lifestyle of giving for the benefit of others and working to meet their needs instead of your own each and every day. It is an active choice that must be made daily. And it is a core leadership principle.

> *To have true influence, you must embrace a lifestyle of*
> *giving for the benefit of others . . . It is an active choice that*
> *must be made daily. And it is a core leadership principle.*

Giving of yourself is not a sure path to poverty. It's not about holding a garage sale under a "Free" sign. I am not even referring to the traditional giving of money, clothing, or food for charity. What I am referring to is a lifestyle choice, embracing the abundance mentality, and the belief that we are all part of something bigger than ourselves.

Hopefully, by this point in the book, you have broken through the walls of self-preservation. Therefore, giving yourself away should be a natural act, as you have moved into a relational mindset. When you give of yourself, you will gain—but that is not the focus, just the reality.

HOW DO YOU BECOME A TRUE INFLUENCE WHEN YOU HAVE BEEN TAKEN ADVANTAGE OF MANY TIMES BEFORE?

In the Bible, there is a famous dialogue between the Apostle Peter and Jesus. Peter asks how many times he is supposed to forgive people around him. "Seven times?" Jesus's response is amazing: "No, seventy times seven." He then points out that God's grace is deep and God forgives us consistently in our weaknesses. Therefore, practice forgiveness aggressively.

Practice forgiveness aggressively.

To give it all away means to shower mercy upon people who don't deserve it and grace upon those who think they do.

Real Influence

Let me explain how this works by telling you about a very good friend of mine, Larry Green. Larry is a giver. We call him a sherpa because he never asks for anything but instead tries to help us grow. His needs are always met, in many ways. There are scores of men and women, like me, who count Larry as one of the most significant influencers in their lives.

Larry's story is revealing. It begins with a man rising up the corporate charts only to become less and less fulfilled, and more and more dissatisfied. Does this sound familiar? He was doing a good job as a valuable executive at one of the world's largest companies just seven years ago. Yet he was stuck on something: himself. Larry was insecure, and because he didn't know who he was, he didn't know how to give of himself. The "What I do" was overpowering the "Who I am."

Yet today, Larry is the most confident and humble man you will ever meet, and he knows exactly who he is. He now helps other leaders figure out who they are. Larry tells them that what they do is irrelevant, because what they do stems from who they are. I am one of the many people who have benefited from Larry's wisdom.

What is interesting about Larry is not really his process—though there is one—but rather the style of his leading and influencing. Larry just simply . . . is. He takes the lessons he has learned and the hard roads he has walked and provides perspective, wisdom, and hope to hundreds of leaders every week. Simply put, Larry gives away everything he has been given—and I don't mean money or clothes or food. (Though he does that too.) Larry gives away everything truly important that he has received: wisdom, encouragement, perspective, and discernment. In return, his bucket is filled up on a regular basis. His giving gives him so much that you can feel it when you are around him. It makes you want to follow in his footsteps.

True Giving

The most valuable gifts that you can bestow upon the world are the ones inside of you—the real you. Have you ever been mentored? What about encouragement from a parent, a teacher, a coach, a friend, a relative, or a boss? Can you give that away? Have you earned wisdom the hard way, and could you share it? Give that wisdom away!

Giving yourself away may not sound very appealing at first, but once you free yourself from protecting your own interests, it's amazing how liberated you'll feel as a serial giver. Before I began giving myself away, I went through an internal battle. While I felt like I should be doing more for others, I still had the desire to serve my own ambition.

Arguably the most influential person to ever live was Jesus Christ. There is a great story about his apprenticeship process for his vagabond trainees, the apostles. He told his disciples that he was going to send them into villages to help people. The twist was that he wasn't going with them. He then told them something strange:

"As you go into these cities to help people, I don't want you to take money or clothes." In essence, Jesus was telling his disciples to travel light. Then he told them to give away everything they had that had been given to them.

So, let's get this straight: don't take anything with you . . . but give everything away? Exactly! Give everything that you have been given. The lesson Jesus taught those men that day is part of the reason for his continued influence today. It is a replication model for influencing others.

The Ultimate Gift

My friend the lieutenant general told me an inspiring story about a heroic young private who gave the ultimate gift to his fellow soldiers. Ross McGinnis, who grew up in a small Pennsylvania town, became a gunner in the US Army right after high school. He was later deployed to Baghdad during the Iraq War. He was a .50-caliber machine gunner in a hatch atop a Humvee during a mounted patrol in Adhamiyah on December 4, 2006, when a grenade was thrown into his vehicle during an attack. He yelled a warning to the four soldiers inside the Humvee through their wireless radio system, but instead of leaping out of the vehicle to save himself, McGinnis threw his back over the grenade, pinning it between his body and the Humvee's radio mount, absorbing the deadly blast.

Private First Class McGinnis was just nineteen years old when he gave his life for his friends in a selfless act of heroism. The US Army awarded him its highest decoration for bravery, the Medal of Honor, as well as the Bronze Star and Silver Star medals. He was buried in Arlington National Cemetery.

Later the general told me about the funeral and how much impact Private McGinnis's actions have had on the entire US Army. Here are the powerful words of a proud father about his son who gave the ultimate gift:

> Ross did not become our hero by dying to save his fellow soldiers from a grenade. He was a hero to us long before he died, because he was willing to risk his life to protect the ideals of freedom and justice that America represents. He has been recommended for the Medal of Honor . . . That is not why he gave his life. The lives of four men who

were his army brothers outweighed the value of his one life. It was just a matter of simple kindergarten arithmetic. Four means more than one. It didn't matter to Ross that he could have escaped the situation without a scratch. Nobody would have questioned such a reflex reaction. What mattered to him were the four men placed in his care on a moment's notice. One moment he was responsible for defending the rear of a convoy from enemy fire; the next moment he held the lives of four of his friends in his hands. The choice for Ross was simple, but simple does not mean easy. His straightforward answer to a simple but difficult choice should stand as a shining example for the rest of us. We all face simple choices, but how often do we choose to make a sacrifice to get the right answer? The right choice sometimes requires honor.

Person of Peace

PFC McGinnis is a model for selflessness as well as heroism. I am asking you to consider becoming a leader of influence by sharing your gifts selflessly with others. Business leaders often respond to that request by noting that people have taken advantage of them when they've done selfless things in the past. I first learned this from Mike Breen, a British author and speaker who is a leader to leaders around the world. Mike taught me to think differently about those I serve by looking for those called "persons of peace."

You should give of yourself to those individuals who are "people of peace," which means those who are open to receiving what you have to give. When you find someone who is open to receive, then you simply give freely of whatever you have that is needed. If someone is hostile or selfish, you don't give, you move on. Influence typically occurs when a person is open to it because of respect, need, or desired gain. If a person with bad intent crosses your path, just move on. Don't fret or worry, simply move.

After my wife and I moved our family from Oklahoma to Atlanta, we met many business and community leaders in our new city. One of those men was J. T. Robinson, an amazing business consultant at Chick-fil-A. J.T. spends his days helping Chick-fil-A franchise operators grow their businesses and their leaders.

On our first meeting together, I was struck by his sincerity in offering to help us get to know Atlanta and its leaders. What we didn't realize at the time was that we were "people of peace" for him. In our first six months in Atlanta, J.T. helped us dozens of times in a variety of ways, giving us advice on people to meet, restaurants to frequent, and sights to see, while also introducing us to many new friends within Chick-fil-A. I was flabbergasted by his generosity with his time and network of contacts. I made it a goal to serve him in the same way that he has served us.

We experienced true influence from someone who gave of himself to serve us. Since then, we have forged a great friendship based on mutual respect and service. J.T. helped connect GiANT with Chick-fil-A, an alliance that will benefit hundreds of thousands of people annually through the Chick-fil-A Leadercast event (www. chickfilaleadercast.com), which is the largest leadership broadcast in North America.

It has occurred to me that someone looking at our relationship from the outside might think that we are trying to "outgive" each other. The reality is that we are giving ourselves to a friendship in unselfish ways; the best possible relationship. We are serving each other through our relationship so that giving becomes natural. I encourage you to try this with a trusted friend. Over time, you won't be conscious of giving, you'll just be glad for the opportunity to share because it is so fulfilling.

What to Do with Competitors?

I'm in the leadership business. There are many other leadership training companies out there. Technically and practically, they are my competitors. Yet I have no qualms with sharing information and advice to serve their needs. It is also true, however, that many of my competitors don't share my service orientation and nonthreatened view of competition.

The key to living as a giving influencer is to exude a giving attitude that becomes contagious. I have found that people are often disarmed by my openness. Some competitors find it confusing and unnerving. Others embrace the opportunity to share an abundance mentality.

My approach to my competition is not learned, it is inherited. My mother handed down this gift. My parents owned two flower shops, and whenever a competing shop owner would say something unkind about ours, my mother would insist, "Don't give them what they want. If someone says something negative, just ignore it and be your nice self. It will be like salt in a wound."

My mother had a natural instinct for serving others. She made customers in her shop feel like valued guests in her home. She focused on serving them rather than worrying about the competition. My mother taught me to give freely and to let the competition bark all it wanted.

So how do you give? Here are five practical ways to give yourself away without losing yourself:

1. Give up ownership of yourself—This is the best gift you can give yourself and your family. Besides, if you agree with me that we have a Creator, then what He has created is His, not yours.
2. Understand the value of your gifts—Each of us has amazing attributes and gifts. Each skill, talent, and gift is worth something to you and to others. Recognize and be grateful for the value of your gifts and share them as treasures.
3. Realize where the gifts came from—Did you get the power to think from an MBA program? I don't think so. Your gifts and talents come from your Creator, your parents' DNA (also from our Creator), your experiences, and from the influences in your life. You are the recipient of all these gifts, so sharing them should come naturally!
4. Give up self-pursuit—The crazy pursuit of material things or status is never truly fulfilling, but when you give freely of yourself, the fulfillment often far exceeds anything you could have imagined.
5. Practice giving yourself away—There is no formula. You simply start. Practice freely by sharing your knowledge, your wisdom, and your experience with others who are open to it. The only secret here is not to be pushy but rather to be interested in serving the real needs of others first.

Leadership comes alive when you focus on the mission and the people over yourself.

This chapter explored how to influence others. The process, which can be learned only through practice, takes time. To be a true influence is to focus first on relationships before seeking opportunities, and to give of yourself without expecting rewards. If you do these things, you will benefit in many wonderful and unexpected ways.

CHAPTER 9

NO RISK, NO REWARD

Most people think of driving a car as a task, a necessity, and not usually a pleasant experience. I live in Atlanta, where traffic is often bumper to bumper, so I tend to agree with that view. But recently my friend Eric Gregory introduced me to driving as an exciting and entirely pleasurable experience by allowing me to borrow one of the beautiful machines from his Motor Cars of Georgia auto dealership in Atlanta.

This was my James Bond dream car: an Aston Martin V12 Vantage Roadster. *Wow* is the only word to describe my driving experience behind the wheel of this incredible automobile. I found an open roadway and discovered that driving can be far more than just traveling from one place to the next. In the Aston Martin, driving was a thrill ride, an adventure, and a totally fulfilling experience.

Leading with influence will affect you in much the same way. It transforms routine business and personal interactions into thrilling adventures and fulfilling experiences. When the rubber meets the road for a leader of influence, when you give freely of your gifts day in and day out, your life takes on so much more meaning and gives you so much more pleasure that you'll wish you'd never lived any other way.

I don't own an Aston Martin that I can drive every day, but thankfully, I do have the gift of influence that has made my life a much more enjoyable ride. That's the great thing about the giving of yourself to others. When the relationship is one of giving freely, it isn't draining. Instead it charges you up and gives you a new level of experience.

The key is to take every interaction with a team member, a co-worker, a friend, or a family member and transform it into something special; something deeper and more meaningful than either of you expected.

A dear friend once called me to ask for help and advice. He is an executive, and the pressure of the job was stressing him out. He wanted to get away for some peace and reflection, so he asked my advice on executive retreats. When he called, I was preparing for an international business trip. I was rushing around to prepare for that trip, and I could have offered him a couple of quick recommendations, but I sensed that he needed more than that.

This was an opportunity to give of myself, to be of service, and to exercise true influence. So I put aside my own preparations and focused on my friend and what he needed from me. I chose to be significant and to create a memorable experience for him. Over several hours, I created for him a retreat kit made up of a letter, a personal three-page story written just for him, a music CD, and three books that addressed his concerns about the stress of leadership in times of crisis.

Now, there was some risk in this. I was giving up valuable time to put in more effort than my friend had really asked for. He might have decided that I was a total nutcase for giving so much beyond the book recommendations he'd requested. Yet I was honored that he'd come to me, of all the people he knows, for assistance in a tough time. I could sense that he needed more than just a book. So I took the plunge and served his needs rather than my own.

The risk paid off. My friend thanked me for what I'd done, but over the next few days, his gratitude increased as he went through the materials and found how helpful they were to his situation. For four days, he texted me and emailed me, not just thanking me but sharing with me how the materials helped him find a way to deal with the stress that had been weighing on him. Instead of thinking I was crazy, he was highly appreciative for the time and energy I'd given to serving his needs.

My executive friend came back from his retreat a changed man. It was noticeable and evident then, and it still is today. My little risk paid off in an amazing way. While this experience was about him, it also benefited me. He was grateful, and our bond of trust was strengthened. My cup filled up as I saw how my efforts paid off for him and for our relationship as well.

If I hadn't put myself out there and risked overreacting to his request, I would not have seen or felt the reward. You too have the opportunity to experience the rewards of influence every day in ways both big and small, but always fulfilling. In order to experience them, though, you will have to put yourself out there by risking a little to gain a lot.

Imagine a young businessman asking an older executive to meet for coffee. The younger guy was full of angst and needed encouragement. His mentor could have thrown some quick advice and an inspiring word or two, but that was a short-term solution. He wanted to serve the young leader's long-term needs. So he listened with the intent to not only hear his words but also to understand his feelings. Then, based on both his words and feelings, he asked the stressed-out young guy a series of questions, guiding him through a process where he could find his own answers and feel good about the journey.

The conversation ran much deeper than either had anticipated. The young man became emotional at one point, but he was grateful for the time and thoughtfulness so graciously given him. What helped him most was to realize that the issue weighing so heavily upon him was something that most of us go through as we mature in our business and personal lives. He found peace that day, and a deep bond was formed between the two men.

After hugging and thanking his mentor, the younger man called his new wife to tell her about the incredible experience he'd just had. Over the next few years, he and the older executive talked often, sharing their experiences and resources, enriching each other's lives.

The mentor found their exchanges exhilarating. The young man's energy and enthusiasm was contagious. They also shared a strong spiritual foundation, and as their relationship grew stronger, so did their bond of faith. They prayed for each other, and they prayed together. He came to regard the younger man as a son or little brother.

Each man benefited from this relationship in ways that can't be measured. Each man energized the other. I know because I was this young man when I reached out to an extraordinary businessman, John Bingaman, who became this caring and authentic mentor to me.

Johnny has had success in both the health care business and in real estate development. Yet his true successes have come in his investment in men like me. There are dozens of them. Each time I would visit his home, we would sit in his comfy den or at the back patio with a glass of lemonade. I would be tensely sharing my pains and gains, and he would diligently listen and offer the best advice imaginable at the time.

Each time I met with Johnny, I received so much wisdom and encouragement. I think that Johnny would tell you that he has benefited from our relationship too. We encouraged and supported each other. I am so grateful for the influence John has had in my life. He will forever be a hero to me.

This is just one example of the rewards of serving others first. John Bingaman and I no longer live in the same city, but I still think of him often. His influence is in my memory, and now I get to share it with you!

The rewards of influence are:

- You encourage others in your life to find peace and fulfillment.
- They come to trust you, and a chemistry develops between you.
- You become relevant to their needs, and they see you as credible and important to their lives.
- They move beyond self-preservation mode as you reach out to them.
- You bring significant and memorable insights into their lives.
- They receive your insights and ask more of the relationship.
- You continue to give of yourself for their benefit, and they realize it.
- They express their gratitude and begin serving you, without being asked.
- You serve them in positive ways.

- They give you respect and speak highly of you.
- Each time you leave each other, you are energized and grateful for the relationship.

The reward comes through the process of giving. Having true influence means that you are intentional in your impact. Most of the leaders I know who have been significant in my life have been successful in their careers. I attribute this to their desires to reach out and build trustworthy relationships. Their real success comes in sharing their gifts and giving of themselves to benefit others.

When you help others more than yourself, your life will flourish.

Action No. 7: Become Significant in Your Impact

Who would you say are the five most significant people in your life? Think of them right now. Why are they so important to you? What did they do to become so valuable in your life?

In my experience, we value others as significant for these types of reasons:

- "She listened to me."
- "He was always there for me."
- "I just value his opinion."
- "She was kind to me and lifted me up when I needed it."
- "They always seemed to know what was best for me."

Do these examples ring true for you and those you value as significant in your life?

Let's explore these significant relationships a bit. Make a list of those who have enriched your life in some way. How did each of them become significant for you?

While some on your list may be a relative or a dear friend, I am certain that their influence on you was not just some random occurrence. If you look at those who are truly significant in your life, they most likely had someone who served them just as they served you. Each of them had to

- grow in character as he or she learned how to trust and become trustworthy;
- become credible in competency;
- learn how to become intentional in motives;
- break through fears and self-preservation;
- pursue relationships in the midst of opportunities;
- share gifts with others;
- learn how to be significant with memorable impact.

The point is that the significant people in your life are on their own journeys too. They are working on themselves, most likely with the help of others to be a benefit in the lives of others.

Developing true influence is a lifelong process. True influence is a lifestyle that doesn't operate on a time schedule. To become influential and to have impact in someone else's life means that you must be willing to be impacted and influenced along the way.

Significant Leadership

Obviously, you want to be an influential leader, or you wouldn't have read this far. The influence model offered some changes you could make to have a more positive impact and a more fulfilling life.

One of my closest friends is a British leader named Steve Cockram. Our wives and kids really enjoy one another. It is a great friendship because we all connect so well. My wife even calls Steve her brother. What I appreciate most about Steve is his desire to be significant in the lives of others. He is one of the most significant influencers in my life. His own successes and failures have helped him become a better leader over the years. Yet Steve is most valuable to me because he too is a work in progress.

Steve was mentored by a brilliant leader, Mike Breen, whom I mentioned earlier as an influence on my life. But it goes further than that. Steve submitted to a true apprenticeship with Mike to become the best leader possible. What has occurred is amazing. I have watched Steve grow exponentially and become a teacher to others, helping other leaders do the same.

Steve is now apprenticing others, and, thus, the process continues. No stone is left unturned as every area of life—from character to competence to influence—is touched. The amazing thing is that I benefit just by observing and talking about his amazing growth. Steve offers a fresh perspective, and he is a good listener. Every time I am with him, I grow. I value that immensely. Because of my business, I am around some amazing people. Steve influences me as much or more than anyone. Here is what he has done for me:

- established trust;
- shown himself to be relevant;
- been willing to work through tough stuff;
- listened when I needed it;
- challenged me when I needed it;
- sought to build a relationship without asking me to do anything for him;
- given of himself consistently.

Are you willing to be a true influence? Are you willing to live it and show it? To be significant is a great gift to others and to yourself.

Impact

My company is called GiANT Impact because something that has an impact tends to be permanent.

When you think about a meteor colliding with the Earth, that is big impact. When you think of a ding in your car door, that is small impact. In both cases, the marks tend to remain for the duration. I'm convinced that we make marks (impacts) on people, both positive and negative. I would just as soon they be positive marks, wouldn't you?

Situations and individuals both can impact your life. Typically, to impact someone means that the experience is memorable. It becomes the long-term memory that could show up later in a journal or biography. That is impact. To be significant means that we intend to impact the lives of others.

All great leaders have at least one significant influence in their lives, and at least one significant impact moment. When you read the biographies or autobiographies of men and women you admire as leaders, look for those influencers and impact moments. I find it amazing to see how both positive and negative influences made significant impressions and shaped them.

Now imagine yourself as one of those influencers in a historical leader's life. Do you realize that every great leader had an everyday leader who had a significant impact on him or her? In fact, that person most likely had not just one but many influencers!

Since having an impact can change or alter the lives of others, we can actually be significant in the lives of future leaders by making the effort to serve others today.

Ramifications of Influence

For most, money is probably the first thing that comes to mind as a reward. Yet the best rewards are typically not financial. Here are examples of common rewards for leaders of influence:

- Having other people name their children after them.
- Goodwill, which is the outward appreciation of internal influence.
- Referrals or business opportunities.
- An enhanced reputation, which is the natural badge of honor awarded for living a life of influence.

While these are just a few in a long list of potential rewards for a life of true influence, there is one reward that surpasses them all. Most rewards are given to us by others. There is also an internal reward, though, for significant influence. That reward is self-fulfillment, which I've noted throughout this book. To know that you have been a gift to someone is fulfilling. This realization is only the beginning, though. Knowing that you are significant in another person's life also leads to better sleep, lower blood pressure, a lighthearted attitude, less stress, and, ultimately, peace.

Peace is the end reward of influence. Fulfilled leaders give of themselves to serve people with the best intent. Peace becomes the ultimate reward for the person of true influence. And peace is worth more than gold or silver.

Peace is the end reward of influence. Fulfilled leaders give of themselves to serve people with the best intent.

Reward Incorporated

Rewards are not only for individuals. Organizations can gain the rewards of influence as well. Appreciation can carry over to both small and large companies, nonprofit organizations, school systems, and churches. Customers reward good service.

When I list the following organizations, what comes to mind? Are there any on this list that rank high for their customer service, inspiring customer loyalty?

- Target
- Walmart
- Salvation Army
- Delta Airlines
- Southwest Airlines
- Marriott Hotels
- Ritz-Carlton
- Amazon
- Apple
- Habitat for Humanity
- Samaritan's Purse
- CNN
- Fox News

Companies and brands that inspire loyalty are usually those that put the customer first. Your patronage is their reward, and it pays big dividends in positive word of mouth, referrals, and brand loyalty. What were your thoughts as you read through the list above? Which of those businesses or brands have earned your loyalty and patronage? We reward those who have influence in our lives.

One of our leaders at GiANT, Chris Ediger, is a devoted fan of Steve Jobs's Apple products. Maybe I should say he's a fanatic. He is devoted to the brand, and he rewards Apple with great loyalty and word-of-mouth recommendations. His enthusiasm is contagious, and now I have the Apple bug too. Quality products and service build up compound interest, and I'm proof of that. That is how the reward works. When you do the right things the right ways, you gain the benefit of the right rewards.

Chick-fil-A

One of the best examples in American business of positive influence reaping big rewards is the restaurant chain Chick-fil-A. For more than sixty years, this company has been a model for quality service. This fast-food chain has more than 1,500 stores in thirty-eight states, and its numbers just keep growing, thanks to an unusually loyal and appreciative customer base.

Quite simply, Chick-fil-A is appreciated. When it enters a market, the whole community receives a boost because the DNA of the organization is geared toward community service. The leader and founder of this brand, Truett Cathy, has a mantra that puts a high priority on service: "Customers will make us bigger when we get better."

Through the years, Chick-fil-A has improved gradually and in stages, while always emphasizing great standards in the quality of its fare and impeccable service inside. Recently, it has moved into a new stage of impact by serving as an example of influence in the lives of its customers.

What does a chicken chain have to do with leadership and influence? The short answer is that it models the behavior that its people admire. I have seen it firsthand. I have watched the video of one operator who created a daddy-daughter date night to encourage fathers to be leaders in their families and communities. I have seen operators lead initiatives to serve schools and communities and even entire regions. Not only that, but the company is leading initiatives to help people live healthier lifestyles. That is true influence.

For a restaurant chain that is closed on Sundays, one of the best days for food sales, Chick-fil-A is doing just fine. Why? The rewards of influence. Its customers reward this fast-food chain with respect and loyalty. The company is focused on giving, on relationships, on serving, and on excellence. It is not focused on the rewards, but the rewards are certainly being reaped.

In fact, Chick-fil-A has a sort of friendly competition with its customers, with each trying to outgive the other. Chick-fil-A strives to exceed the usual standards for food quality and customer service in the fast-food industry. Customers reward that effort by becoming raving fans and telling others about the company. There is tremendous value in that approach to business.

It is very possible to mimic Chick-fil-A's influence model. If you are a business owner, you could set up your company to be a similar influence in your community. What would happen if you actually implemented that model? How would that change your employees, your business, and your life?

The best business leaders understand that they don't rest on their laurels. The best never rest. They are too busy giving!

The great reward of excellence is more business. The great reward for intentionally serving communities, families, and individuals is long-term respect, which can't easily be diminished. Companies can build up capital with customers. Yet the best business leaders understand that they don't rest on their laurels. The best never rest. They are too busy giving!

Mutual Trust

The reward for living a lifestyle of influence is the gift of mutual trust. When you serve and give of yourself and reward another person, you establish a covenant bond of respect and appreciation, and make a rare and powerful impact.

The reward for living a lifestyle of influence is the gift of mutual trust.

Our company strives for this every day. I know hundreds of leaders who live the same way. I have seen it with my own eyes. And yet it is not something that happens to those leaders on autopilot.

To gain the reward of mutual trust requires a lifestyle of high character, trustworthiness, competency, and credibility. You have to constantly seek to progress together toward shared goals. And because of the capital of trust built up between both parties, it becomes easier to accomplish more and more over time.

Mutual trust is achieved when each person breaks through the walls of self-preservation and strives to be a positive influence, while making a significant and memorable impact on a regular basis. This powerful relationship is emotionally satisfying and mentally stimulating, allowing for the achievement of shared goals.

The Influence Economy

The process of influence and impact works like the economy. In fact, it *is* an economy, of sorts. There is a supply of influence and a demand for influence. Everywhere you go, people want to be encouraged or helped or served in some way.

The process of influence and impact works like the economy. In fact, it is an economy, of sorts. There is a supply of influence and a demand for influence.

As in financial markets, people exchange influence in every relationship. The exchange of appreciation, reputation, or goodwill takes place every time someone impacts someone else. One person pays out, another collects, and then passes it on. This cycle of giving and receiving goes on every day.

The influence economy can be seen in partnerships, marriages, friendships, and families. The payout of service "buys" us significant influence on one another. When this commerce occurs, better things than money change hands. Appreciation, gratitude, and good wishes become reciprocated by the significance of impact.

I think that is the way it was set up from the beginning. Humans were given skills and talents from God to give away to others for their mutual benefit and the greater good. Gratitude and appreciation flow back and forth throughout the process.

To be influential is to be a part of a bigger economy. You and I are simply participating for the benefit of others.

Trajectory of Influence

To help you understand how important influence is, I would like to finish this chapter by offering some perspective on the impact your influence can have on other people. Put on your physics cap, if you have one, and think for a moment about the concept of trajectory: the path of an object moving in space.

While I don't advocate that anyone be flung into the cosmos, I am suggesting that every leader affects the trajectory of those around him by his actions and words, either positively or negatively. If you were to draw a map of your own history, you would notice that your trajectory was impacted by those who influenced you for the good or for the bad. This point really comes into play when you consider that you have undoubtedly impacted the paths of others. We all do.

It happens in business as well. Kevin Murray is cofounder of CTR Partners, a commercial real estate company located in Duluth, Georgia. He and his partners realized that they have the opportunity to set up their business so that each one can have the greatest impact based on individual talents and skills. Kevin is a true positive influence. His intent is always to bring out the best in others. So he spends most of his time working one on one with leaders, encouraging other influencers.

CTR Partners serve as a platform for encouragement, positive impact, connections, and goodwill. In return, the company is rewarded by supportive relationships. While the business is doing well, relationship accounts are overflowing! The partners live out significance as an offering of their company.

Because of this commitment to relationships and influence, CTR has gained influence with leaders across the country. This small company feels larger than life because it is willing to risk itself for others. Kevin and the others receive the rewards daily—sometimes in little doses, sometimes in large doses.

Say Yes

The ultimate reward of influence is a fulfilled life. You will experience fulfillment when you embrace a lifestyle of serving others first. Positive living, thriving business, and fulfilled mission are only a few attributes to this lifestyle. I saw the truth in this while sitting in a restaurant in the JW Marriott Hotel in Shanghai, China. A sharp American woman executive enthusiastically greeted two business colleagues and then turned to introduce them to her guest. Her comments revealed her respect for her colleagues and the depth of their mutual respect.

"Mr. Li, let me introduce you to two of my favorite people," she said. "These two gentlemen have worked with me over the last five years. They are not only smart but are also the most trustworthy men I know."

She was beaming as she brought them together, and I could tell that their respect was genuine. It is possible to work with others in a covenant bond. It is possible to truly respect and trust one another. It is possible to be an influence in the lives of others and to be impacted positively by them in return.

There is a reward for this lifestyle of influence. You and I simply must choose to engage by taking the risks necessary to obtain the rewards. If you choose to pursue money and other short-term rewards before building relationships and true influence, you risk leaving much of your true value on the table. But when you choose to be a positive influence for the betterment of others, the money will follow, and your priorities will be in the right order. You must take risks to reap the rewards of influence and see your leadership come alive.

CHAPTER 10

WHY YOU PROBABLY WON'T DO THIS

Take this as a challenge. Influence is difficult, and most leaders never reach the levels of significant influence because their instincts for self-preservation are too strong. Is it time for you to break through to become a true and positive influence?

Turn on the switch: the impact switch that is hidden somewhere inside your heart. When you flip the switch, your influence will spread, and your world will begin to change. It's time to develop your plan for influencing your world, starting with yourself.

Remember, leadership is about influence. Influence is power. And how you use that power will affect your world and those around you. Will you choose to empower or overpower? To liberate or dominate?

These are the questions you must answer. You affect and alter the trajectory of all those around you—those you lead and those you live among. The courses of other people's lives, as well as your own, can move toward the positive or negative. The decision is yours.

True influence comes to you when you change yourself to change the world. The framework I've provided will help you to know yourself and your intent so that you can overcome the powerful instincts of self-preservation. Once you have broken through to serve others first, you can then build relationships before seeking opportunities. This results in a lifestyle shift that will have positive ramifications for years to come.

Please realize this: when you choose to give yourself away, you will inevitably receive as much or more than you give. When you give away influence with the goal of impacting others positively, you are rewarded with fulfillment and significance, peace and joy.

You will be blessed with meaningful relationships and even more influence. When you embrace this lifestyle, you will also come to appreciate and enjoy another key figure in your life: you!

You Must Choose

If you have made it to this point in the book, then you are most likely one of three types of people.

- You are already a true influence, and this book has served to remind you of key points, while providing you with tools to help others become true influences.
- You know that you have the potential to be an influencer, but the daily stress of your job and other demands of life have held you back from fulfilling your potential. You just need a booster shot to energize you.

- This is your first exposure to these concepts. You are intrigued and excited about undertaking a new journey to a better life, and that is exciting!

No matter where you are in life, think of yourself as if you were just beginning the journey of influence. Picture yourself getting inside an old Douglas C-47 Skytrain, used primarily in World War II to launch the 101st Airborne division to victory. The plane has a nostalgic feel to it as you climb aboard with your gear firmly attached. You see the jumpmaster standing at the front of the plane. He begins marching back and forth as the last jumper gets situated. The instructions are:

1. "Stand at attention when we are over the drop zone."
2. "Lock in when I tell you to."
3. "Jump when you see the green light and hear my voice saying 'Go.'"

You memorize the instructions. Though they are easy enough, your heart is racing. The plane's engines fire up, and you move toward the drop zone. Everyone else is either looking down or glancing around nervously. You know what to do. You have been preparing for this moment for months. You go through your checklist one last time. It is loud and windy in the plane. The jumpmaster has opened the door. Your heart feels like it will beat out of your chest. It is almost time.

Just then, everything slows down. You hear the bark of the drop sergeant telling the troopers they are over the drop zone. Everyone stands at attention. It's time to lock in. You take your tether and lock into the jump cord with the other jumpers. There is no turning back now. In a matter of minutes, you will be flying through the air and focused on your mission.

All eyes are on the light over the door. You can see clouds zooming by as the red light glares. Then it happens: the red light switches to green. You hear the words you have been waiting for: "Go! Go! Go!"

You shuffle like penguins toward the open door. You can see the leaders ahead of you jump into the vast skies. It is your turn. You look to the jumpmaster beckoning you forward. You take one last step and fling yourself out of the plane.

At that moment, things change. It is a different world. The roar of the engine is replaced by silence, except for the whistle of air rushing through your gear and past your ears. Then you feel the tug as your parachute opens and your descent is checked. Your free fall becomes a controlled float toward the surreal landscape below. You've been taught that landing is the most crucial part of parachute jumping. It makes sense. While most people are afraid of the jump, it is actually the landing that can bring the most damage. A rock, a tree, or simply too much speed can break bones—or worse.

You hit the ground and roll, and your chute descends upon you, covering you. Shedding the material, you see the other troopers landing in similar fashion all around you. You made it! From gearing up, to climbing on, to locking in, to jumping. You made it.

So it goes, too, with the life of true influence. The door of influence is normally always open, yet the timing of influence is crucial. I have had to learn to wait for the right moments before jumping. Green means go. Red means stay. It is an exercise in discernment.

Paratroopers know the risk before they board the plane. Yet they still lock in and jump with the understanding that they could suffer in the process. They could be shot, they could miss the drop zone, or they could land high in a tree with no way down.

To be a true influence is similar to parachuting out of a plane. You need to understand the risks. You may be perceived as being too personal. You may not connect with people in the way that you'd hoped. You may be shot down by comments from the person you are trying to help. Yet the benefits of the mission are far greater than the risks.

For those engaged in jumping, the door is always open and the call to serve others is always there. You simply need to await the green light with an understanding of how to handle the potential pitfalls of influence. To be a true influence is to be all in.

What If You Don't?

"But what if I don't want to?" some have asked.

To be a significant influencer is a choice. You can say no or you can say yes. There are consequences for your decision, though. To say no is to join the lines of leaders everywhere living their lives for their own purposes and gaining the rewards and ramifications of that lifestyle. There is nothing wrong with it on paper, except that it is a severely limiting life. To say yes to a life of influence is to say yes to watching amazing things happen to people you have influenced and receiving the rewards of that impact. It is a far better way to live.

Many people miss the joyful opportunity of seeing others succeed. Many never feel appreciated for being significant in another person's life. If you never try true influence, you may never escape the daily drudgery of life.

When your focus is solely on your own needs, you live a transactional existence, which means that most of your relationships are transactional, or one-way. You take, but you do not give. Nor do you receive.

You have a choice. You can live on that lonely path or you can walk with trusting and grateful companions who share your desire to have an impact and to be part of something bigger than themselves.

A Better Way

I want to encourage you to walk with true influence, joined by those who share your selfless mission. It is so much more fun! There are scores of people who can attest to it. Oklahoma City social entrepreneur Lance Humphreys is one of those who has chosen to be a true influence—so much so that he schedules his days around those he can help. Here is a quick look at the things he is involved in:

- Creating a company called Bloom that helps single mothers have meaningful employment in a safe environment while they meet their family obligations.
- Serving under-thirty leaders as these young people grow into significant influencers.
- Coaching leaders across the country who want to maximize their influence and significance within their communities.
- Participating in the building of a new type of lake community based on relationships, agriculture, and design. He is creating a rural-urban community in the middle of Oklahoma to help people connect while they relax.

Lance makes his living around his role as an encouraging influence to leaders. He and his family have dedicated themselves to serving as role models and encouragers for leadership in their community. Understand this: a true influencer values mission and performance together. Lance is a brilliant businessman and a significant leader.

A true influencer values mission and performance together.

An example of Lance's influence is the encouragement he has given Tim Ulrich, a young developer from California who moved to Oklahoma City to overhaul the worst areas of the city. Lance has served Tim, who is serving many of the poorest in the Oklahoma City area.

Tim has taken the worst street and completely overhauled what was considered by most as old, broken, and dangerous. Today he offers the poor opportunities to grow, to earn respect and to have an apartment that is safe.

Lance is committed and intentional about using his life to serve others. Tim lives the same lifestyle. Together these two guys have received the reward of great relationships with friends and influencers in Oklahoma City and across the country.

To be intentional about influence is the best way to live. I thoroughly believe that you can change your world to match your mission and desire to influence. I have seen too many people give up too quickly on influencing others because they fear losing something instead of daring to give up everything.

Several years ago my wife, Kelly, and I decided to do things differently when it came to relationships. We built an apartment in the basement of our home and invited our business guests to stay there instead of in a hotel. We host more than a hundred nights a year in the "Kubicek Chalet." Vendors, authors, speakers, partners, and future employees stay in our home.

There are several strategic reasons for this. Instead of being away from home a hundred nights a year or more while hosting visitors, I can be with my family and introduce our guests to our lifestyle. Our kids, Addison, Will, and Kate, enjoy the privilege of meeting some of the most amazing people. It helps them learn how to deal with adults and gives them perspectives that most kids don't get to experience. This approach gives our guests a real view of our family. They can see that we are definitely the real deal when it comes to living the lifestyle we advocate.

Each night usually ends with some relational time on our deck or in my study, which wouldn't happen if the guest stayed in a hotel. Thus, we bond more quickly. My kids have stories upon stories of individuals who have impacted their lives. We even have regulars who look forward to our time together, as we do with them. By the way, the Kubicek Chalet is free to guests, which is a bonus!

The Lifestyle of Influence

True influence is our lifestyle, and it should be yours too. It becomes both *who* you are and *what* you do. Your life will be liberated and all about benefiting others. Yours will become a relational life versus merely a transactional one. To be influential is to be intentional, available, and willing to impact—not just in business but also in all of life.

To be a true influence, you must understand how to have a positive impact on those around you in every area of your life.

You've read about the basics of influence and how to overcome self-preservation instincts by breaking through and reaching out, but how do you teach someone else to become significant and memorable? First it is important to understand that every person, every family, and every organization can influence the lives of others. The model is the process of relating, learning, breaking through, and giving away. It is about being, acting, and investing. To be significant and memorable is highly rewarding.

Most successful people I know struggle with some form of guilt about not giving enough, which they can alleviate by serving others and being significant in the lives of everyone they meet. Some leaders I've known have made millions of dollars only to realize that money truly doesn't buy happiness. When they search for fulfillment, many realize that making a positive impact in the lives of others may bring them the happiness they seek.

The problem is that it is hard for them to simply become significant overnight. It usually takes years for them to understand who they are. Most of these people try to be significant by focusing on giving money, thinking that charity will lead to fulfillment. The reality, though, is that the game has changed for them, and they don't know the rules. Success for them is transactional. They've always felt that for them to win, someone else must lose. You attain significance by impacting others with positive influence and freely sharing your gifts by giving yourself away. Is it possible to be both successful and significant? Certainly!

Imagine what it would look like for a group of leaders to define success as being true influences. What if they built a platform to significantly impact and benefit others? That group of leaders could change companies, communities, and maybe even a nation. The larger the platform, the more influence could be made.

Creating Memories

True influence is memorable. We all remember those who've had a positive impact on our lives—anyone who has given above and beyond our expectations. Memorable moments of influence are gifts for a lifetime. They inspire gratitude. They can happen every day if you want them to. True influence doesn't happen without giving of yourself. As you open up your life and your organization to become a positive influence, you will experience pleasure as well as some pain. It is not easy to give or serve or influence. But it is worth it.

> **HOW DO I TRAIN MY LEADERS AND THOSE WHO WORK FOR ME TO BE A POSITIVE INFLUENCE?**
> Start by talking about it. Make time to discuss. Use the influence model to discuss where you are with each other. What needs to be improved, and where can others excel? Take your lunch hour and learn strategy. You may want to pick one chapter or go chapter by chapter through the book. The influence model is a great visual to use to discuss internal relationships and client or customer relationships. It specifically helps your team know exactly where they stand with others as it relates to character and competency.

In an earlier chapter, I mentioned Booster Enterprises as a company that exhibits character and competence. Its leader, Chris

Carneal, is skillful at creating memories for his team and for those around him. Here are some practical ways that Chris combines memories and influence in his leadership style:

- Every December, Chris creates a photo album of the top events of the year, organized by month. This process allows him to remember and celebrate the key moments of the year with his team, which helps build morale
- After every meeting with a client or potential client, Chris writes a memorable thank-you note and delivers it either on the spot or very soon thereafter. The key here is that he trains every person who works for him to do the same thing.
- Every major event is filmed by an amazing video-design group to capture moments and create videos to be used online, inside the company, and for recruiting.
- Each proposal made by his team is an experience. Each is fresh and memorable, which is a tribute to the growth culture that Booster Enterprises has created.

To celebrate his employees' successes and to build company culture, Carneal organizes two retreats per year with his one hundred or so team members. Each retreat unites and energizes the company, reminding everyone of their vision, mission, and values. This time is used for rest, culture building, and applauding team members who have excelled and grown as leaders in the previous months. Their award ceremonies are some of the most affirming I have ever seen.

There are several more amazing ways that Chris creates memorable impact. The key is to take good ideas and implement them into your plan to influence those you lead and serve.

Your Plan

What is your plan for influence? How will you structure your life to influence your organization, your family, and your friends? The idea of creating an intentional plan is nothing new. The problem with most of us, though, is that a plan can feel restrictive and cumbersome. We remember the many New Year's Eve resolutions that we have failed to keep after only a few weeks.

Over the past few years, our company has assisted in developing these plans for our clients, their teams, and their organizations. The beautiful reality is that every person and company is different, and their needs are specific. Therefore, the concept of being intentional can be customized to the specific needs of a group of people.

To do this, it is vitally important to be intentional in the following areas:

- being intentional with time;
- being intentional about improving your influence;
- being intentional about team and organizational growth;
- being intentional with your personal growth.

In today's leadership culture, there is a general lack of holistic thinking when it comes to the growth of influence. The tendency in our society is to place leader development in the hands of intellectual lecturers and anemic training programs. Today's leadership cultures are typically defined by a best-selling book brought in by an influencer. While nothing is inherently wrong with this, it does limit the overarching growth of leadership potential in an organization.

What is missing are continuity, strategy, and perspective. The truth is that each of us wakes up every morning with priorities in mind, whether we are cognizant of them or not. These priorities typically revolve around pain resolution, or putting out fires. We are then met with the hope of a better tomorrow. Therefore, the whims of our daily "pains" and "gains" take precedent over any calculated plan for growing both the capacity and capability of leaders.

This brings us to your process of growth. To grow, you must be intentional. To be intentional is to build the proper tools and the correct system for your personality. Here are some questions to get you started.

1. Know yourself—What do you need to do to know yourself?
   * Do you know your DNA/personality wiring?
   * Do you understand your capacity constraints?
   * Are you leveraging your strengths?
   * Do you know your purpose?

2. Lead yourself
   * Do you know how to stop yourself from making poor choices?
   * Do you partner with others to compensate for your weaknesses?
   * Are you responsive or defensive?
   * Do you understand the power of humility versus the detriment of pride?

3. Know others
   * How well do you know your core leaders or those who are close to you?
   * Would *they* say that you know them?
   * What can you do to know them better? What about the little things?

4. Influence others
   - What is your style of influence?
   - How do others want you to lead?
   - Have you considered being more innovative in your routines or your methods for communicating?

5. Know your team
   - How well do you really know the culture of your organization?
   - Are you open to knowing it better?

6. Influence your team
   - What is the style of your organization?
   - Who is the best influencer in your organization today?
   - What does that person do well?
   - How should you change what you do?

7. Know your customer
   - What are the different segments of customers in your world?
   - If you had to label the different customer types, how would you describe them? Create a term for each.
   - How well do they want to be known?

8. Influence your customer
   - What could you do to make a customer's world better?
   - Get your team involved. How could the organization positively influence your customers?
   - What could you do within the community to be a true influence company?

Impact

The end goal of influence is to have positive impact in the lives of others as you achieve fulfillment. Most people don't think about their impact on the world until near the end of their careers and lives. Why not be intentional about making an impact now by concentrating on a lifestyle of influence? To help you do this, write down what you would like your family and friends to say about you at your funeral many years from now. Then consider what they might say about you if you died today. What is the margin between what they would say today and what you would want them to say later?

Spouse:
Children:
Parents (if applicable):
Business partners:
Colleagues:
Employees:
Friends:
General public:

The end goal of influence is to have positive impact in the lives of others as you, yourself, achieve fulfillment.

The gap between what they would say now versus what you want them to say in the future could be very telling. This is by no means an effort to get people to say nice things about you. Rather, this exercise is meant to give you perspective on what you may need to change in your approach to your relationships.

Again, I can name countless executives who are wonderful at home but tyrants at work. Conversely, there are hundreds of leaders who use all of their energy at work and drag home a tired, lifeless person to their family. True influence is 24/7. It means that you are willing to know yourself and to work on yourself, so that you can lead yourself at work and at home.

"To Be Known" (The Known Problem)

I believe that one of the core human desires is to be *known*. To be known means that someone invested time and energy to learn who you are. In essence, it means that someone values you enough to want to know you and to accept you for who you are. This desire is not a weakness or a fix for insecurity issues. The best leaders I have ever been around have invested time in knowing their people. With that knowledge comes appreciation. This type of leader inspires others to relate to others and lead them at higher levels.

This beckons the question "Who do you really know?" How many people would say that you truly know them? That you have invested time and energy, selflessly, to understand and appreciate them? There is a direct correlation between those who believe that you are for them and those who believe you know them. They go hand in hand. Conversely, how many people really know you? One, five, ten, or more? How many people could say that they know you from the inside out?

Many people who suffer from depression believe that no one knows them or cares about them. It is a debilitating reality. People want to be known. And yet, being known is a two-way street. It is a process of being open with others and investing in them too.

Now you are ready to be a positive influence in other people's lives. Let's review your action plan for making leadership come alive in you:

Action No. 1: Give trust to become trustworthy.

Action No. 2: Become credible, not just smart.

Action No. 3: Be intentional in your influence.

Action No. 4: Break through your walls of self-preservation.

Action No. 5: Pursue relationship before opportunity.

Action No. 6: Give yourself away.

Action No. 7: Become significant in your impact.

The Life of a Leader

This book began with the death of a leader, Paul Tatum. It is fitting to end it with one of joyous life. The stories I've shared are meant to awaken those searching for more fulfillment, to encourage those seeking to energize, and to equip those training others to influence. My near-death experience led to liberation. My business perspective changed, based on the life and death questions I asked and answered. That experience changed my life forever. I learned, over time, that what I gained through this experience was much greater than what was lost physically or financially.

My new life began when I freely gave of myself to influence others for their benefit. I have learned to pursue relationships solely for the joy of helping others fulfill their missions in life. My near-death experience was not the end but rather, the beginning. While I was recuperating at home, my oldest daughter,

Addison, came in from gathering the mail. Her sweet voice whispered, "I love you, Daddy."

Her loving words made me grateful and helped me overcome the pain of staring at bills that would pile up along with the excessive fees that the meager Mexican hospital had charged. All of the money I'd saved for my start-up business went to pay for my emergency surgeries and my hospital bills.

The game of real life began.

The last letter in the stack of bills and other mail included a letter from our first client we had yet to serve. As I opened it, I was amazed to find not only a note but a check. Our first client, whom I had influenced and encouraged for months before any formal business relationship had started, wrote:

Jeremie,

I am so excited to work with you at GiANT. I hope it is okay to pay you six months in advance for tax purposes. Looking forward to it,

Steve

The check covered the costs of my start-up, replenishing all that had gone to my medical bills. A tear ran down my cheek when I saw that check and realized what it meant. My faith had been rewarded, and so had my belief that giving freely of my gifts to others is the best way to live.

I was rewarded for building a relationship before seeking an opportunity. The rewards did not stop there. We faithfully served this client for years, and now Steve Hatfield and his Blusource team faithfully serve us as our distribution warehouse partners out of Oklahoma City.

Life happened. I began believing in others. My leadership came alive because I was more focused on them than me. My influence then began to grow and I found a much more fulfilling life, one that I am grateful for each and every day.

Make your leadership come alive. Everyone will benefit, including you.

INTERVIEW WITH DAVID SALYERS OF CHICK-FIL-A

I had the opportunity recently to interview David Salyers, Chick-fil-A vice president of marketing, on a trip to the World Expo in Shanghai, China.

David is an amazing leader and an excellent influencer. He is one of the most passionate guys I know. We are so excited to partner with him, Dan Cathy, and the entire Chick-fil-A family with the CFA Leadercast.

Here is an excerpt from that interview:

QUICK FACTS ON CHICK-FIL-A
- The first Chick-fil-A was founded in 1967 by Truett Cathy.
- As of 2010, the company has approximately 1,500 stores.
- Chick-fil-A has stores in 38 states.
- Total employee, owner-operators, and associates as of 2010: approximately 70,000 systemwide.
- Retention rate of headquarters staff and operators: 97 percent.

DAVID, HOW IS CHICK-FIL-A SERVING ITS CUSTOMERS OUTSIDE OF THE RESTAURANT?

Influence within Chick-fil-A is simply an extension of our positive influence to our seven to ten million customers each week. Just as we care about our employees, we also care for our customers. That extends to our customers' health and their families. Most people want something from their customers. Chick-fil-A wants something *for* our customers. That is a paradigm shift for most other companies.

WHY IS CHICK-FIL-A FOCUSED ON INFLUENCE IN THIS SEASON OF THE COMPANY'S LIFE?

You cannot be a positive influence in your customers' lives if you don't do the basics right. We must continue to produce a great chicken sandwich and a great service atmosphere. That is our first focus. Yet we also know "to whom much is given, much is required." So we believe that influence is the next extension of quality and service. We simply want to give back to those we serve.

WHAT DOES THAT PRACTICALLY LOOK LIKE?

Here are some examples that we are excited about:

- Chick-fil-A Leadercast—We have partnered with GiANT Impact to create the largest leadership simulcast to the everyday leaders within over five hundred communities in North America. The goal is to encourage and equip these leaders as they serve within their communities. This event is a great example of the type of creative influence we desire to promote through live events and simulcasts.

- Daddy-Daughter Date Nights—Local operators have created daddy-daughter date nights to help fathers connect with their daughters. We simply help them pull it off. As soon as they get out of the car, we create a red carpet experience with a table host and flowers for the girl. We provide a great meal with a photo and dessert. We even help the dads with talking points so they can more easily connect with their daughters.
- Father-Son Campouts—At various locations, operators have created annual father-son campouts to help dads connect with their sons by hosting an all-night campout at a Chick-fil-A restaurant. They play games and pitch tents in the parking lot. In the morning, they finish by having breakfast in the store.

All of these events and programs are just the starting place to what we want to do in the future. The fun part about this is our spirit of partnership both with companies that help us execute these and our customers who volunteer alongside our employees. These influence initiatives are community events, not corporate programs.

WHAT DO OTHER COMPANIES NEED TO DO TO LAUNCH CAMPAIGNS OF THEIR OWN?

My advice would be to live it first. You cannot give what you don't possess. If a company wants to positively influence their community, they need to be authentic and do the basics well. Secondly, influence programs are not Return On Investment projects. We are not doing these as a marketing initiative but truly to benefit our customers. We realize that our core is excellence, then service, followed by customer connection. Once a company has established these, then they can go to influence. I would challenge people to do these well and then get as creative as possible. Our world needs a lot more positive influence.

DAVID, ANY OTHER THOUGHTS ABOUT INFLUENCE?

Yes. We believe that influence is about restoration and that our restaurants can actually be places where people can learn to live better, love better, and lead better. It is a process of helping people live up to who they could be. We are simply grateful to be in a place to serve people to become better leaders, parents, and people. We have an anthem that we use to describe our influence initiative. I think it is important to share it so that people can understand how important we view the responsibility to positively influence those you serve. Hopefully, it will give a great perspective of our influence initiatives.

Chick-fil-A's Live. Love. Lead. Anthem

Life is precious.
So I will not exist.
I will not get by.
I will not muddle my way through.
No.

I will Live.
I will cherish every sunrise.
Every heartbeat.
Every breath.
And I will prepare myself for countless more.
I will thank God for my health

By embracing what is healthy.
I will nourish my future
By nurturing my present.
And I will respect the gift that is my life
By inspiring others to do the same with theirs.
I will Live.

And I will Love.
I will be a better father.
A better mother.
A better spouse.
A better friend.
I will sacrifice my time and myself
Only to realize it was no sacrifice at all.
I will not be an absentee anything.
My commitment will be unmistakable.
My compassion boundless.
And my joy contagious.
I will Love.
And as a result, I will inspire others to love too.

I will Lead.
I will lead as a servant.
By example and by faith.
Not seeking glory
But humbly giving it.
I will pursue integrity.
Follow wisdom.
And treasure fun.
I will encourage.

Influence.
And inspire others to lead as well.
I will walk ahead of you.
I will stay beside you.
And I will stand behind you.

I will Live. I will Love. I will Lead.
And because I will, I will inspire others to do the same.

FIND THE REAL GiANT

At GiANT, we believe that there is a different standard and style of leader needed in the world today. We call this new style of leader a GiANT. Can you find the real GiANT in the story below? Make a game and have some fun.

Let me give you a hint. The real GiANT can be found in the letter *i* in our name. Make the correlation and email me any comments on JeremieKubicek.com.

In the period around 1000 BC, there lived a king who had a predicament that seemed insurmountable at the time. His nation was at war with another. They were hated rivals. Border disputes produced raiding parties, which led to numerous battles for hundreds of years.

In one dispute, the enemy nation gathered troops for an all-out battle on a hill facing the king's country. The king dispatched his troops to an opposing hill. A clay valley was the no-man's-land between the warring nations.

In a typical battle of that period, both war parties would have marched toward each other and engaged in hand-to-hand combat.

In this case, the opposing nation sent one warrior into the valley alone. This warrior was huge, with enormous muscles. He wore bronze armor that made him appear even more ominous as he stood in blazing sunlight coming down from atop the opposing hill.

The warrior stopped in the middle of the valley and, with one look from left to right, yelled out insults at his hated enemy. This man was so much larger than the other men that he felt confident with this challenge: "Pick your best fighter and bring him out to fight me. If he gets the upper hand and kills me, we will all become your slaves. But if I get the upper hand and kill him, you all will become our slaves and serve us. I challenge all of your troops this day. Give me a man. Let us fight it out together!"

The king was terrified and uncertain of what to do. This warrior appeared to be too much for any of his men.

We don't have anyone that big. Our best fighter wouldn't stand a chance, he thought. *What if we just attacked them? Do they have more men like this one?* All of these thoughts ran through his head. He was paralyzed with fear at the thought of being enslaved by his enemy.

It was at this moment that the unlikeliest of figures appeared: a mere boy. The battlefield was no place for such a child, but this particular boy had three brothers who were fighting with the king. The boy's father had sent food with him to deliver to the older brothers. The boy was also a musician, so he'd played for the king. The king valued him as an entertainer and errand boy but regarded him as a nuisance and liability on the battlefield.

The boy had watched as the fierce warrior challenged his king's entire army. Full of bravado, and fearless, the boy mocked the boastful warrior and encouraged his brothers and their comrades to stand up to his challenge. When the king heard of the boy's actions, he sent for him.

The broad-shouldered king was a warrior himself; one of his nation's best fighters. But his faith and courage were depleted. Fear had taken hold of him. On this day, he was neither a Dominator nor a Liberator.

"Master," the boy encouraged the king, "don't give up hope. I'm ready to go and fight."

The king wanted to have hope, but this boy was too young and inexperienced to take on the fearsome warrior waiting in the valley.

Still, the king had heard stories of this shepherd boy killing a mountain lion that had attacked his sheep. He was fearless. The king thought that his small size might disarm the warrior and his fierce courage might allow him to take the overconfident enemy by surprise.

"Prepare him for battle."

No soldier's armor would fit the lanky boy. The king put his own bronze helmet on the lad and handed him his own sword. He looked ridiculous! He could hardly walk under the weight of it all.

The boy removed the helmet and put down the sword.

"I don't need it," he said.

The shepherd boy grabbed his staff. On his way down to the valley, he stopped at a creek and selected five smooth stones, putting them in his pocket. As he approached the looming warrior, the boy produced a sling—a mere pouch of leather on two strings. He put one of the heavy stones in the sling.

The warrior observed this with amusement. He wore more than 120 pounds of armor that no stone could penetrate. His spear was like a fence rail: the forged steel tip itself weighed over 15 pounds. He taunted his scrawny foe and the king who'd sent him.

"Am I a dog that you throw me a little stick?" asked the warrior. "Come on, I will make road kill of you all! I will turn you into a treat for the field mice!" He continued to curse the boy and the entire opposing army.

The boy did not waver and returned the boastful threats with his own. "You come at me with a sword and spear. I come at you in the name of God, the God of these troops, whom you curse and mock. This very day you will be handed over to me."

The warrior screamed out and ran at the boy. The boy raced toward the massive warrior. The king watched from the hill.

As he came within range of his much bigger foe, the boy began swinging his loaded sling with a skill achieved through many hours of practice while shepherding his flock in the fields. He wound the sling in the air and then let the rock fly with all the power he could muster. His stunned enemy had no time to react. The stone hit the warrior just below his steel helmet, embedding itself in the exposed flesh of his forehead. The mighty soldier collapsed, first to his knees, then face first to the ground, shaking the valley floor with his dead weight.

The enemy warrior was dead. Once his supporting soldiers saw him fall, they fled like herds of frightened gazelles, dropping their shields and armor. The king and all his men took heart and gave chase, forcing the enemy troops well back into their own territory.

As you undoubtedly surmised, this is the biblical tale of the boy David, King Saul, and the infamous warrior giant Goliath. David eventually became king, replacing a leader whose instincts were to protect himself and his power and position first.

David represents Liberator leaders everywhere. The more you

learn of his life, the more you see the empowering nature of this leader and the standard he set for all leaders from that time forth.

Goliath, obviously, represents the Dominator: the boisterous bully who tried to use sheer force to overpower the nation of Israel. Like most Dominators, he was given what he deserved.

Saul represents the middle ground: the self-protecting leader. If you study the life of Saul, you will find that on some days he was a Liberator, and on others, a Dominator. David was his savior on the battlefield that day; he brought down Goliath. But on several occasions, later in his life, Saul tried to kill David out of jealous rage. The real issue for Saul was that he always put his own interests first. He was afraid to empower and liberate, and so, at times, his insecurity caused him to overpower and dominate. He represents the inconsistent middle of the leadership spectrum.

Who is the Real GiANT?

It is for this reason that GiANT exists. We believe that the humble, responsive leader is the one with real influence. As a company, we are dedicated to encourage and resourcing responsive leaders.

ABOUT GiANT

G iANT Impact is an influence company. Our mission is to improve the leadership culture of America (and ultimately the world) by transforming the standard and style of leaders from pride-based leadership to humility-based leadership. Personal leadership change is as important to us as organizational culture change. We work on both.

We serve hundreds of thousands of leaders annually in a myriad of ways. Some leaders leverage our events and our resources to grow their organizations and leaders, while others focus on utilizing our programs to impact their communities. That is great with us. We often ask people to leverage us.

Every company is great at some things and average at others. We are really good at awakening leaders and fueling them to impact others. We also understand how to help organizations grow through higher levels of leaders. We use events, experiences, and long-term leadership programs to help both individuals and organizations grow.

Examples include:

- Chick-fil-A Leadercast—This global broadcast and live leadership exhibition in Atlanta is the premier global leadership broadcast, highlighting a highly creative forum of experts, everyday leaders, and special guests. It is an awe-inspiring event that starts many down their first leadership road or refuels the long-seasoned leader. You can host these amazing events in your community via live broadcast by going to www.chickfilaleadercast.com.

- Catalyst—This brand is focused on the under-forty, next-generation leader. Yes, we said "under forty." Don't be surprised if you get carded at one of our dozen or so events. This brand produces some of the freshest content and experiences in the world today. Visit www.catalystspace.com to get a strong overview of this vibrant movement.

- Intentional Leadership Initiatives—We believe that leaders need to be stretched to grow. So we have created some impactful programs, assessments, resources, and experiences that benefit individual leaders, departments, and organizations as a whole. We have years of experience working in both large and small organizations. The size of the company is not as important as the openness and willingness of the leadership to make things happen. We value initiative more than credentials. Visit www.giantimpact.com to see a highlight our programs.

- Inspiring Content—We like to encourage, because that is what we do. Our teams are highly creative, and we are constantly innovating with new content and thought. If you would like to follow me on this journey for fresh, encouraging content, then come join me for free at www.jeremiekubicek.com. I realize the name is hard to spell. Talk to my parents on that one.

- Other GiANTs—We have a number of GiANT companies with the same mission. GiANT Partners helps grow companies specifically by serving the executive leadership team through strategic growth plans (www.giantpartners.biz). GiANT Capital helps entrepreneurs and middle-market companies with creative financial analysis so they can continue to grow (www.giantcapital.com).

- International Impact—A few years ago, we founded GiANT Experiences to take our customers and leaders that we serve on international adventure trips to influence and impact entrepreneurs in other countries. Wow, is all I can say! We are now taking amazing trips with other influential leaders who have a desire to give. What happens is a wholesale change in worldview and a new perspective on life. Come go with us at www.giantexperiences.org.

The best way to describe our focus is this: if *we* wouldn't want to go to one of our events, we simply don't do them. If we wouldn't buy our own resources, then we are simply wasting everyone's time and money.

At GiANT, we are committed to changing the world by changing ourselves first. Allow us to serve your journey to change your world and those that you lead every day. Awaken your influence so that leadership can come alive again.

If you are interested in joining our team, you may want to know this: At GiANT, we value trustworthy character, relevant competence, and significant impact.

We are an organization that affects both the head and heart of the leader. Just by the sheer nature of our approach to leaders, we tend to attract people who are givers, who are servant leaders. Servant leaders are those who tend to view their place in the world as, if you will, that they are here for a reason other than perks and a big paycheck; that they are really here to serve those around them, and they have an opportunity to do that at GiANT.

Most of our programs are designed to help these individuals grow their company with less stress and a little more fun, but primarily position them in such a way that they truly can become a servant leader to those around them. Most CEOs and business leaders actually get so busy trying to grow the organization that they have difficulty unwinding from that to do what they really want to do, which is, in most cases, serve those around them. Our job is to help them do just that.

If this is you, then we'd love to talk. You can reach us at info@ giantimpact.com.

While we work with world-class leaders and influential groups, we truly value the everyday leaders who are working night and day to make things better in their companies, in their schools, and within their communities.

A new style of leader is emerging: leaders who are for others before themselves. Leaders who will give themselves away for others. GiANT serves those types of leaders to create something far greater than simply a business.

Join us in changing the landscape of leadership from a domination mind-set to a liberation culture. We are looking for leaders within every community in America to commit to breaking through their own walls of self-preservation and then encouraging and equipping other leaders within their scope of impact.

ACKNOWLEDGMENTS

I want to especially thank my wife, Kelly, and my kids, Addison, Will, and Kate, for giving me the grace and time to write this book. Even more, I want to thank them for living lives of impact. I love our family.

To Chris Ediger, thanks for your partnership and friendship. You are a loyal partner and a consistent sounding board for the vision. I so appreciate your role and your belief in me. Thanks for putting in the hours.

Thanks also to all GiANTs. Beth Lostumbo, you are such a help to me and my family. Thank you for serving us so well. To all of the ATL GiANTs and Catalysts, thank you for working so hard to expand a vision and to serve so many influencers around the world. Your work is valued and valuable.

To my board, thank you Rich Christman, Pattye Moore, Collin Sewell, and Matthew Myers, for believing in me and for challenging me to capture this influence model for others to know. That was a pivotal board meeting. I value each of youI am grateful to my GiANT partners: Matthew Myers, for your consistent friendship and lifelong partnership; David Woods, for your belief in the GiANT vision. Ray Sanders, you are truly the man; thanks for the voicemails of encouragement. Dan Bales, your partnership is special. To Dave Rae, for your help in helping reach the mission—together. To Louis Upkins, for your amazing partnership. You are that brother I never had. To Mary, Andrew, Brent, and the rest of the OKC team, thank you for believing in the message and mission. To those who have also invested in the mission of GiANT, thanks for all you do. Special appreciation to David Gillogly, Brian Banks, Bond Payne, Ralph Mason, Brian Hill, Ron Harris, Kent Humphreys, Dick Horton, and many others.

I want to acknowledge my friends who continue to add so much value in my life. Chris Carneal, for your inspiration and enthusiasm. You are a great friend. Lance Humphreys, your years of counsel and support are a godsend. Steve Cockram, your counsel is strategic and always spot-on. I am so grateful for our friendship. Brandon Hutchins, you are a constant encourager. Ryan and Carmel Litz, not only have you been with us in thick and thin, but we know you always will be. J. T. Robinson, you are the man. Thanks for giving yourself away!

Thank you for the many influencers in my life over the years. You are both friends and partners in influence. Thanks to Mike and Kianna Kubicek, Larry Green, John Bingaman, John Cragin, Hance Dilbeck, Regi Campbell, Gary Parsons, Kent Humphreys, Rocky Hails, Odus Compton, and Sonny Newton.

To Chick-fil-A, thank you for your partnership. I especially want to thank David Salyers, Dan Cathy, L. J. Yankosky, Lauren Thigpen, Tim Toussopolous, and Steve Robinson. Your example is amazing.

To the Booster Nation, thanks for Changing the World and for being for me. I am so for you!

The following people have helped me so much in the process of writing and thinking about writing. Thanks to Dr. Rusty Ricketson, Kevin Murray, Dr. Jerry Patengale, Adam Wren, Pat Lencioni and the Table group team, Brett Trap, Dr. Henry Cloud, Eric Hill, Dr. Jarrod Spencer, and Jeff Tennyson.

Special thanks to you, Shannon. Shannon Marven is a great agent via Dupree Miller. Thank you for believing in me and for allowing me to dream. That is crucial.

Also, Becky Nesbitt, you are a rock star. Special appreciation to Jonathan Merkh and Howard Books/Simon & Schuster. I appreciate your team effort. Also, Jason Young, Daniel Decker and Wes Smith, you guys are good at what you do. Thanks for your hard work and creativity.

To my YPO blokes, thank you for a great forum. Jeff Lamkin, Kevin Bailey, Charles Douglas, Chris Ray, and Ben Morris: you have helped me more than you know.

One more shout-out to all of the influencers along the way: Bridgeway (Ryan and Adriane especially); Global Options friends (we shared many stories together); Waterdeep and Don Chaffer; Jules, Lindy, and EB—you all are special! To my future friends, thank you as well.

Finally, to those who are willing to influence and risk yourself to serve others, thank you. This book is meant to help you equip and encourage others. Leverage it to empower others.

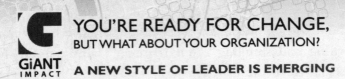